Homosexuality

Other books in the Issues on Trial Series

Homosexuality

Robert Winters, Book Editor

GREENHAVEN PRESS

An imprint of Thomson Gale, a part of The Thomson Corporation

Detroit • New York • San Francisco • New Haven, Conn. • Waterville, Maine • London

Christine Nasso, *Publisher*
Elizabeth Des Chenes, *Managing Editor*

© 2007 The Gale Group.

Star logo is a trademark and Gale and Greenhaven Press are registered trademarks used herein under license.

For more information, contact:
Greenhaven Press
27500 Drake Rd.
Farmington Hills, MI 48331-3535
Or you can visit our Internet site at http://www.gale.com

LIBRARY OF CONGRESS CATALOGING-IN-PUBLICATION DATA

Homosexuality / Robert Winters, book editor.
    p. cm. -- (Issues on trial)
    Includes bibliographical references and index.
    ISBN-13: 978-0-7377-2793-7 (hardcover)
    1. Homophobia--Law and legislation--United States--Cases. 2. Homosexuality--Law and legislation--United States--Cases. 3. Sodomy--United States--Cases. 4. Same-sex marriage--Law and legislation--United States--Cases. I. Winters, Robert, 1963-
    KF4754.5.A59W56 2007
    342.7308'7--dc22
                                                                    2007017020

ISBN-10: 0-7377-2793-4 (hardcover)

Printed in the United States of America
10 9 8 7 6 5 4 3 2 1

Contents

Chapter 1: States Can Outlaw Sodomy

Chapter 2: Gay People May Not Be Singled Out for Discrimination

Chapter 3: Sodomy Laws Are Unconstitutional

Chapter 4: The Question of Same-Sex Marriage

Foreword

The U.S. courts have long served as a battleground for the most highly charged and contentious issues of the time. Divisive matters are often brought into the legal system by activists who feel strongly for their cause and demand an official resolution. Indeed, subjects that give rise to intense emotions or involve closely held religious or moral beliefs lay at the heart of the most polemical court rulings in history. One such case was *Brown v. Board of Education* (1954), which ended racial segregation in schools. Prior to *Brown*, the courts had held that blacks could be forced to use separate facilities as long as these facilities were equal to that of whites.

For years many groups had opposed segregation based on religious, moral, and legal grounds. Educators produced heartfelt testimony that segregated schooling greatly disadvantaged black children. They noted that in comparison to whites, blacks received a substandard education in deplorable conditions. Religious leaders such as Martin Luther King Jr. preached that the harsh treatment of blacks was immoral and unjust. Many involved in civil rights law, such as Thurgood Marshall, called for equal protection of all people under the law, as their study of the Constitution had indicated that segregation was illegal and un-American. Whatever their motivation for ending the practice, and despite the threats they received from segregationists, these ardent activists remained unwavering in their cause.

Those fighting against the integration of schools were mainly white southerners who did not believe that whites and blacks should intermingle. Blacks were subordinate to whites, they maintained, and society had to resist any attempt to break down strict color lines. Some white southerners charged that segregated schooling was *not* hindering blacks' education. For example, Virginia attorney general J. Lindsay Almond asserted, "With the help and the sympathy and the love and respect of the white people of the South, the colored man has risen under that educational process to a place of eminence and respect throughout the nation. It has served him well." So when the Supreme Court ruled against the segregationists in *Brown*, the South responded with vociferous cries of protest. Even government leaders criticized the decision. The governor of Arkansas, Orval Faubus, stated that he would not "be a party to any attempt to force acceptance of change to which the people are so overwhelmingly opposed." Indeed, resistance to integration was so great that when black students arrived at the formerly all-white Central High School in Arkansas, federal troops had to be dispatched to quell a threatening mob of protesters.

Nevertheless, the *Brown* decision was enforced and the South integrated its schools. In this instance, the Court, while not settling the issue to everyone's satisfaction, functioned as an instrument of progress by forcing a major social change. Historian David Halberstam observes that the *Brown* ruling "deprived segregationist practices of their moral legitimacy. . . . It was therefore perhaps the single most important moment of the decade, the moment that separated the old order from the new and helped create the tumultuous era just arriving." Considered one of the most important victories for civil rights, *Brown* paved the way for challenges to racial segregation in many areas, including on public buses and in restaurants.

In examining *Brown*, it becomes apparent that the courts play an influential role—and face an arduous challenge—in shaping the debate over emotionally charged social issues. Judges must balance competing interests, keeping in mind the high stakes and intense emotions on both sides. As exemplified by *Brown*, judicial decisions often upset the status quo and initiate significant changes in society. Greenhaven Press's Issues on Trial series captures the controversy surrounding influential court rulings and explores the social ramifications of

such decisions from varying perspectives. Each anthology highlights one social issue—such as the death penalty, students' rights, or wartime civil liberties. Each volume then focuses on key historical and contemporary court cases that helped mold the issue as we know it today. The books include a compendium of primary sources—court rulings, dissents, and immediate reactions to the rulings—as well as secondary sources from experts in the field, people involved in the cases, legal analysts, and other commentators opining on the implications and legacy of the chosen cases. An annotated table of contents, an in-depth introduction, and prefaces that overview each case all provide context as readers delve into the topic at hand. To help students fully probe the subject, each volume contains book and periodical bibliographies, a comprehensive index, and a list of organizations to contact. With these features, the Issues on Trial series offers a well-rounded perspective on the courts' role in framing society's thorniest, most impassioned debates.

Introduction

The gay rights movement has often provoked outrage, passion, and highly charged political battles. Even so, the struggle for same-sex marriage seems to have unleashed a backlash comparable in some ways to the right-to-life movement that appeared after *Roe v. Wade* struck down abortion laws in 1973. When in 2004 the Supreme Judicial Court of Massachusetts found that it was unconstitutional to deny marriage to gay couples, it brought the issue to a head.

Opponents of same-sex marriage rushed to place state constitutional amendments forbidding the practice on ballots throughout the country. Generally these laws have passed overwhelmingly, often bringing people to the polls who might otherwise have stayed home. That in turn has benefited some conservative, usually Republican, candidates for Congress and may even have tipped the balance toward the election of George W. Bush in the 2004 presidential campaign. Bush himself promised to work for a federal constitutional amendment that would define marriage as a union between one man and one woman.

At the same time, the issue has shifted the debate over gay rights in some significant ways. Traditionally, opponents of homosexuality have focused on behavior and lifestyle. For them, and for many Americans historically, the issue comes down to sexuality and what some consider aberrant conduct. To this day, many gay rights opponents hold that homosexuality is really a choice. Some opponents even liken it to such deviant practices as bestiality, promiscuity, and pedophilia.

Now, the main debate regarding gay rights centers on gay marriage, specifically laws granting people in same-sex unions the same rights as married, heterosexual partners.

Gay Liberation

The gay rights movement itself may have helped delay the recognition of gay marriage. The Stonewall riots of 1969—a series of violent acts of resistance by gays protesting police harassment in New York City—dramatically changed the struggle for gay rights. Previously, the movement had generally tried to appear conciliatory, conformist, and respectful of social norms as a way to counter the public's fears and misunderstanding of homosexuals. After Stonewall there seemed to be a shift in mood.

At this time the word "gay" came into general circulation. Gay pride parades, gay rights demonstrations, and outspoken gay organizations and spokespeople challenged the assertion that straights were normal and gays were not. Many went further, challenging the very idea of normality and questioning many traditional attitudes toward sex.

The gay movement came at a time when the entire nation was experiencing the sexual revolution. Feminists demanded an end to patriarchal notions of the family and marriage and traditional roles of men and women. Gay people benefited from this new willingness to question the mores that had so clearly oppressed them. Far from demanding marriage rights, many rejected the very idea of marriage as an outdated relic of heterosexism and patriarchy. Other causes, especially overturning the sodomy laws that still threatened gay people with jail, seemed both more important and much more feasible at this time.

The Impact of AIDS

The AIDS epidemic of the 1980s had a profound effect on all of these attitudes. Gay men, particularly, felt the impact of this virulent, sexually transmitted disease, and some blamed the disease on the so-called bathhouse culture of promiscuity and anonymous sex. Many in the gay community also found themselves nursing, and too often burying, gay partners. Some discovered the brutal truth that in the eyes of the law, their partnership was meaningless and they enjoyed none of the typical rights granted to married, heterosexual partners, such as hospital visitation, inheritance, and the right to make legal and medical decisions concerning their loved one. In the wider community, AIDS also provoked deep feelings. For some it was a vindication that gay sex was dangerous, dirty, and a violation of the laws of God and nature. For others, it was a revelation. Suddenly, sons and brothers, even fathers and husbands, were dying of the "gay disease." It also took the life of secretly gay movie star Rock Hudson, who had appeared in films and on television as the epitome of normal, wholesome manliness. It was harder and harder for mainstream society to argue that gay people were so completely different that normal rules and rights simply did not apply to them.

A Changed Society

All of this may have laid the groundwork for same-sex marriage, but it is an issue with which the gay community continues to struggle.

Gay activism, gay suffering, and gay visibility have changed attitudes. While some people still oppose gay rights and reject homosexuality altogether, society has reached a consensus that gay people should not be jailed or ostracized simply for being gay. There are still obvious exceptions, such as the refusal to let openly gay men and women serve in the armed services. There are still closeted actors, athletes, and politicians who fear, with some justification, that coming out would fatally damage their careers. However, the near-universal fear and loathing of homosexuals that existed in the 1950s appears to have come to an end.

The question for many is whether same-sex marriage is a logical outcome of this new acceptance or an unjustified demand that could destabilize society overall.

Marriage as a Right

Proponents of same-sex marriage see it as a straightforward civil rights issue. They argue that just as people once rejected interracial marriage, unfairly and illogically, people now reject gay marriage. There are long-term gay couples, many with children, they state, who need and deserve marriage rights just as much as straight couples.

They advocate for the numerous rights granted to married straight couples, such as health benefits, social security survivor's benefits, and the right not to testify against a spouse. It is unfair and harmful to withhold these from gay couples, they argue.

For them gay marriage is just another hurdle, though admittedly a big hurdle, on the way to full equality for gay people.

Undoubtedly homophobia plays a role in the opposition to gay marriage, but it may not be the only reason for opponents to resist it.

Unlike other gay rights struggles such as those involving antisodomy laws and the don't ask, don't tell compromise in the military, the fight over marriage rights does not simply remove a governmental restriction on gay people. Instead it calls for official recognition of gay relationships, and of gay families—an acceptance that not only overturns legislation but also long-held beliefs and customs. The redefinition of family is disturbing to many, who already feel that the traditional nuclear family is under threat from divorce, feminism, and a culture hostile to family values. Perhaps most significantly, marriage too is defined and bound by religion, which customarily does not recognize same-sex unions. Although proponents demand only the right to civil marriage, leaving it up to individual churches whether to marry gay couples, opponents argue vehemently that a rejection of age-old views of marriage is an assault on the entire Judeo-Christian heritage.

With such strong components as marriage and family, love and sex, and religion involved, homosexuality is inarguably a subject that is likely to stir up deeply personal and emotional arguments on both sides of the political debate.

CHAPTER 1

States Can
Outlaw Sodomy

Case Overview

Bowers v. Hardwick (1986)

In August 1982, police officers went to the home of Georgia resident Michael Hardwick to serve a public drinking summons. With the permission of Hardwick's roommate, they entered Hardwick's bedroom and discovered him engaged in a sex act with another man. They promptly arrested him under Georgia's 1842 antisodomy statute, but the district attorney elected not to prosecute. At that point, Hardwick sued Georgia's attorney general, Michael Bowers, seeking a definitive ruling that the law itself was unconstitutional and invalid, which Bowers refused to do. The suit made its way through the state and federal courts, reaching the U.S. Supreme Court in 1986.

The central question was the constitutional right to privacy, which the Court established in *Griswold v. Connecticut* (1965) when it overturned Connecticut's ban on birth control as a violation of a person's right to privacy. Controversial from the start, the right to privacy was based on the due process clause of the Fourteenth Amendment, and many questioned the Court's reasoning. Those questions turned to very vocal outrage in many places when the Court used the right to privacy as its reasoning to legalize abortion throughout the country in *Roe v. Wade* (1973). For many on the Court, *Bowers v. Hardwick* represented an opportunity to clarify, and possibly scale back, the constitutional right to privacy.

At the same time, gay people throughout the country were growing more visible and more vocal in their demands for equality. Since the Stonewall riots of 1969, gay people had been marching and protesting against discrimination, as well as coming out to friends and family in quieter but no less significant ways. The AIDS crisis, beginning in the early 1980s, dramatically increased both the numbers and intensity of the gay rights movement, as gay people felt they were literally marching for their lives and the lives of their closest friends. Groups like the Gay Men's Health Crisis and the Human Rights Campaign Fund called on gay people to come out of the closet and called on the government to cease treating gay men and lesbians as pariahs and criminals.

In a five-to-four decision, the Court upheld the Georgia law. Justice Byron White, in his majority opinion, rejected any "fundamental right to homosexual sodomy" based on the long history of antigay legislation and attitudes in both Europe and America. In his concurring opinion, Chief Justice Warren Burger went even further, noting that the highly influential eighteenth-century jurist, William Blackstone, could not even bring himself to refer to sodomy except as the "crime not fit to be named" and asserting that a right to homosexual conduct would mean rejecting "millennia of moral teaching." In an equally strong dissent, Justice Harry Blackmun accused the majority of an "obsessive interest in homosexual behavior" and a "willful blindness" to the role of sexuality in intimate human relationships.

The role of Justice Lewis Powell may have been the most interesting. He came down on the side of the majority when it came to the questions of due process and the right to privacy, but speculated that the law's prescribed jail term might violate the Eighth Amendment's prohibition of "cruel and unusual punishments." In 1990, a few years after retirement, Powell publicly recanted his opinion in the case, acknowledging that he had made a mistake, a rarity in the history of Supreme Court justices.

He was not the only one with second thoughts. The Supreme Court of Georgia struck down the law in 1998, in a case involving heterosexual sodomy. Then in its 2003 decision in *Lawrence v. Texas*, the U.S. Supreme Court overturned *Bow-*

ers v. Hardwick, finding that intimate sexual conduct was indeed protected by the Fourteenth Amendment's due process guarantee.

> *"Respondent would have us announce . . . a fundamental right to engage in homosexual sodomy. This we are quite unwilling to do."*

The Court's Decision: States May Pass Laws Against Sodomy Even If the Laws Are Restricted to Sodomy Between Members of the Same Sex.

Byron White

When a police officer found Michael Hardwick in a sexual act with another man, he arrested the couple for violating Georgia's sodomy law. The district attorney declined to prosecute, but Hardwick decided to challenge the law anyway, and his case eventually reached the U.S. Supreme Court. In his majority opinion, Justice Byron White rejected the idea that there is a "fundamental right to engage in sodomy" and the claim that singling out homosexuals for punishment violates their right to equal treatment.

Appointed to the Court by President John F. Kennedy in 1962, White served until his retirement in 1993. Over three decades he developed a reputation as a justice who was extremely difficult to pin down ideologically when it came to civil rights cases. He died in 2002.

Byron White, majority opinion, *Bowers v. Hardwick*, U.S. Supreme Court, 1986.

In August 1982, respondent Hardwick (hereafter respondent) was charged with violating the Georgia statute criminalizing sodomy by committing that act with another adult male in the bedroom of respondent's home. After a preliminary hearing, the District Attorney decided not to present the matter to the grand jury unless further evidence developed.

Respondent then brought suit in the Federal District Court, challenging the constitutionality of the statute insofar as it criminalized consensual sodomy. He asserted that he was a practicing homosexual, that the Georgia sodomy statute, as administered by the defendants, placed him in imminent danger of arrest, and that the statute for several reasons violates the Federal Constitution. The District Court granted the defendants' motion to dismiss for failure to state a claim relying on *Doe v. Commonwealth's Attorney for the City of Richmond*, (1975), which this court summarily affirmed.

A divided panel of the Court of Appeals for the Eleventh Circuit reversed. The court first held that, because *Doe* was distinguishable and in any event had been undermined by later decisions, our summary affirmance in that case did not require affirmance of the District Court. The court went on to hold that the Georgia statute violated respondent's fundamental rights because his homosexual activity is a private and intimate association that is beyond the reach of state regulation by reason of the Ninth Amendment and the Due Process Clause of the Fourteenth Amendment. The case was remanded for trial, at which, to prevail, the State would have to prove that the statute is supported by a compelling interest and is the most narrowly drawn means of achieving that end.

Because other Courts of Appeals have arrived at judgments contrary to that of the Eleventh Circuit in this case, we granted the Attorney General's petition for certiorari [a writ calling for the records of a lower court] questioning the holding that the sodomy statute violates the fundamental rights of homosexuals. We agree with petitioner that the Court of Appeals erred, and hence reverse its judgment.

The Central Issue

This case does not require a judgment on whether laws against sodomy between consenting adults in general, or between homosexuals in particular, are wise or desirable. It raises no question about the right or propriety of state legislative decisions to repeal their laws that criminalize homosexual sodomy, or of state-court decisions invalidating those laws on state constitutional grounds. The issue presented is whether the Federal Constitution confers a fundamental right upon homosexuals to engage in sodomy and hence invalidates the laws of the many States that still make such conduct illegal and have done so for a very long time. The case also calls for some judgment about the limits of the Court's role in carrying out its constitutional mandate.

We first register our disagreement with the Court of Appeals and with respondent that the Court's prior cases have construed the Constitution to confer a right of privacy that extends to homosexual sodomy and for all intents and purposes have decided this case. The reach of this line of cases was sketched in *Carey v. Population Services International*, (1977), *Pierce v. Society of Sisters* (1925), and *Meyer v. Nebraska* (1923), were described as dealing with child rearing and education; *Prince v. Massachusetts* (1944), with family relationships; *Loving v. Virginia* (1967), with marriage; *Griswold v. Connecticut* [1965], and *Eisenstadt v. Baird* [1972], with contraception; and *Roe v. Wade* (1973), with abortion. The latter three cases were interpreted as construing the Due Process Clause of the Fourteenth Amendment to confer a fundamental individual right to decide whether or not to beget or bear a child.

Accepting the decisions in these cases and the above description of them, we think it evident that none of the rights announced in those cases bears any resemblance to the claimed constitutional right of homosexuals to engage in acts of sodomy that is asserted in this case. No connection between family, marriage, or procreation on the one hand and homosexual activity on the other has been demonstrated, either by the Court of Appeals or by respondent. Moreover, any claim that these cases nevertheless stand for the proposition that any kind of private sexual conduct between consenting adults is constitutionally insulated from state proscription is unsupportable. Indeed, the Court's opinion in *Carey* twice asserted that the privacy right, which the *Griswold* line of cases found to be one of the protections provided by the Due Process Clause, did not reach so far.

Precedent aside, however, respondent would have us announce, as the Court of Appeals did, a fundamental right to engage in homosexual sodomy. This we are quite unwilling to do. It is true that despite the language of the Due Process Clauses of the Fifth and Fourteenth Amendments, which appears to focus only on the processes by which life, liberty, or property is taken, the cases are legion in which those Clauses have been interpreted to have substantive content, subsuming rights that to a great extent are immune from federal or state regulation or proscription. Among such cases are those recognizing rights that have little or no textual support in the constitutional language. *Meyer, Prince*, and *Pierce* fall in this category, as do the privacy cases from *Griswold* to *Carey*.

Sodomy Is Not a Fundamental Liberty

Striving to assure itself and the public that announcing rights not readily identifiable in the Constitution's text involves much more than the imposition of the Justices' own choice of values on the States and the Federal Government, the Court has sought to identify the nature of the rights qualifying for heightened judicial protection. In *Palko v. Connecticut* (1937), it was said that this category includes those fundamental liberties that are "implicit in the concept of ordered liberty," such that "neither liberty nor justice would exist if [they] were sacrificed." A different description of fundamental liberties appeared in *Moore v. East Cleveland* (1977), where they are characterized as those liberties that are "deeply rooted in this Nation's history and tradition."

It is obvious to us that neither of these formulations would extend a fundamental right to homosexuals to engage in acts of consensual sodomy. Proscriptions against that conduct have ancient roots. Sodomy was a criminal offense at common law and was forbidden by the laws of the original 13 States when they ratified the Bill of Rights. In 1868, when the Fourteenth Amendment was ratified, all but 5 of the 37 States in the Union had criminal sodomy laws. In fact, until 1961, all 50 States outlawed sodomy, and today, 24 States and the District of Columbia continue to provide criminal penalties for sodomy performed in private and between consenting adults. Against this background, to claim that a right to engage in such conduct is "deeply rooted in this Nation's history and tradition" or "implicit in the concept of ordered liberty" is, at best, facetious.

Nor are we inclined to take a more expansive view of our authority to discover new fundamental rights imbedded in the Due Process Clause. The Court is most vulnerable and comes nearest to illegitimacy when it deals with judge-made constitutional law having little or no cognizable roots in the language or design of the Constitution. That this is so was painfully demonstrated by the face-off between the Executive [the president] and the Court in the 1930's, which resulted in the repudiation of much of the substantive gloss that the Court had placed on the Due Process Clauses of the Fifth and Fourteenth Amendments. There should be, therefore, great resistance to expand the substantive reach of those Clauses, particularly if it requires redefining the category of rights deemed to be fundamental. Otherwise, the Judiciary necessarily takes to itself further authority to govern the country without express constitutional authority. The claimed right pressed on us today falls far short of overcoming this resistance.

Privacy of the Home Is Irrelevant

Respondent, however, asserts that the result should be different where the homosexual conduct occurs in the privacy of the home. He relies on *Stanley v. Georgia* (1969), where the Court held that the First Amendment prevents conviction for possessing and reading obscene material in the privacy of one's home: "If the First Amendment means anything, it means that a State has no business telling a man, sitting alone in his house, what books he may read or what films he may watch."

Stanley did protect conduct that would not have been protected outside the home, and it partially prevented the enforcement of state obscenity laws; but the decision was firmly grounded in the First Amendment. The right pressed upon us here has no similar support in the text of the Constitution, and it does not qualify for recognition under the prevailing principles for construing the Fourteenth Amendment. Its limits are also difficult to discern. Plainly enough, otherwise illegal conduct is not always immunized whenever it occurs in the home. Victimless crimes, such as the possession and use of illegal drugs, do not escape the law where they are committed at home. *Stanley* itself recognized that its holding offered no protection for the possession in the home of drugs, firearms, or stolen goods. And if respondent's submission is limited to the voluntary sexual conduct between consenting adults, it would be difficult, except by fiat, to limit the claimed right to homosexual conduct while leaving exposed to prosecution adultery, incest, and other sexual crimes even though they are committed in the home. We are unwilling to start down that road.

Even if the conduct at issue here is not a fundamental right, respondent asserts that there must be a rational basis for the law and that there is none in this case other than the presumed belief of a majority of the electorate in Georgia that homosexual sodomy is immoral and unacceptable. This is said to be an inadequate rationale to support the law. The law, however, is constantly based on notions of morality, and if all laws representing essentially moral choices are to be invalidated under the Due Process Clause, the courts will be very busy indeed. Even respondent makes no such claim, but insists that majority sentiments about the morality of homosexuality should be declared inadequate. We do not agree, and are unpersuaded that the sodomy laws of some 25 States should be invalidated on this basis.

Accordingly, the judgment of the Court of Appeals is Reversed.

> *"Only the most willful blindness could obscure the fact that sexual intimacy is 'a sensitive, key relationship of human existence.'"*

Dissenting Opinion: Laws Against Sodomy or Other Consensual Sexual Acts Violate the Most Fundamental Rights of Privacy.

Harry Blackmun

In a vigorous dissent, Justice Harry Blackmun, joined by justices William Brennan, Thurgood Marshall, and John Paul Stevens, rejected the Court's contention that Bowers *was only about a "fundamental right to sodomy." Instead, he argued, it was about the right to engage freely in the most intimate relationships possible. He also rejected the underlying assumption that the states had every right to impose either Judeo-Christian morality or traditional mores on their citizens, without some other, legitimate justification.*

Justice Blackmun, a lifelong Republican, was appointed by President Richard Nixon in 1970 and was generally expected to uphold a strict interpretation of the U.S. Constitution. However, in 1973 he authored the majority opinion in Roe v. Wade, *legalizing abortion, and he soon emerged as a staunch advocate for abortion rights and the constitutional right to privacy. He retired from the Court in 1994 and died in 1999.*

Harry Blackmun, dissenting opinion, *Bowers v. Hardwick*, U.S. Supreme Court, 1986.

This case is no more about "a fundamental right to engage in homosexual sodomy," as the Court purports to declare, than *Stanley v. Georgia* (1969), was about a fundamental right to watch obscene movies, or *Katz v. United States* (1967) was about a fundamental right to place interstate bets from a telephone booth. Rather, this case is about "the most comprehensive of rights and the right most valued by civilized men," namely, "the right to be let alone." *Olmstead v. United States* (1928)(Justice Brandeis dissenting).

The statute at issue, Ga. Code Ann. 16-6-2 (1984), denies individuals the right to decide for themselves whether to engage in particular forms of private, consensual sexual activity. The Court concludes that 16-6-2 is valid essentially because "the laws of . . . many States . . . still make such conduct illegal and have done so for a very long time." But the fact that the moral judgments expressed by statutes like 16-6-2 may be "'natural and familiar . . . ought not to conclude our judgment upon the question whether statutes embodying them conflict with the Constitution of the United States.'" *Roe v. Wade* (1973). Like Justice [Oliver Wendell] Holmes, I believe that "[i]t is revolting to have no better reason for a rule of law than that so it was laid down in the time of Henry IV. It is still more revolting if the grounds upon which it was laid down have vanished long since, and the rule simply persists from blind imitation of the past." I believe we must analyze respondent Hardwick's claim in the light of the values that underlie the constitutional right to privacy. If that right means anything, it means that, before Georgia can prosecute its citizens for making choices about the most intimate aspects of their lives, it must do more than assert that the choice they have made is an "'abominable crime not fit to be named among Christians.'" *Herring v. State* (1904).

Majority Ignores the Real Issue

In its haste to reverse the Court of Appeals and hold that the Constitution does not "confe[r] a fundamental right upon ho-

mosexuals to engage in sodomy," the Court relegates the actual statute being challenged to a footnote and ignores the
procedural posture of the case before it. A fair reading of the
statute and of the complaint clearly reveals that the majority
has distorted the question this case presents.

First, the Court's almost obsessive focus on homosexual
activity is particularly hard to justify in light of the broad language Georgia has used. Unlike the Court, the Georgia Legislature has not proceeded on the assumption that homosexuals
are so different from other citizens that their lives may be
controlled in a way that would not be tolerated if it limited
the choices of those other citizens. Rather, Georgia has provided that "[a] person commits the offense of sodomy when
he performs or submits to any sexual act involving the sex or-
gans of one person and the mouth or anus of another." The
sex or status of the persons who engage in the act is irrelevant
as a matter of state law. In fact, to the extent I can discern a
legislative purpose for Georgia's 1968 enactment of 16-6-2,
that purpose seems to have been to broaden the coverage of
the law to reach heterosexual as well as homosexual activity. I
therefore see no basis for the Court's decision to treat this
case as an "as applied" challenge to 16-6-2. . . .

Second, I disagree with the Court's refusal to consider
whether 16-6-2 runs afoul of the Eighth or Ninth Amendments or the Equal Protection Clause of the Fourteenth
Amendment. Respondent's complaint expressly invoked the
Ninth Amendment, and he relied heavily before this Court on
Griswold v. Connecticut (1965), which identifies that Amendment as one of the specific constitutional provisions giving
"life and substance" to our understanding of privacy. . . .

Even if respondent did not advance claims based on Eighth
or Ninth Amendments, or on the Equal Protection Clause, his
complaint should not be dismissed if any of those provisions
could entitle him to relief. I need not reach either the Eighth
Amendment or the Equal Protection Clause issues because I

believe that Hardwick has stated a cognizable claim that 16-6-2 interferes with constitutionally protected interests in privacy and freedom of intimate association. But neither the Eighth Amendment nor the Equal Protection Clause is so clearly irrelevant that a claim resting on either provision should be peremptorily dismissed. . . .

Sexual Intimacy and Individual Choice

The Court concludes today that none of our prior cases dealing with various decisions that individuals are entitled to make free of governmental interference "bears any resemblance to the claimed constitutional right of homosexuals to engage in acts of sodomy that is asserted in this case." While it is true that these cases may be characterized by their connection to protection of the family, the Court's conclusion that they extend no further than this boundary ignores the warning in *Moore v. East Cleveland* (1977), against "clos[ing] our eyes to the basic reasons why certain rights associated with the family have been accorded shelter under the Fourteenth Amendment's Due Process Clause." We protect those rights not because they contribute, in some direct and material way, to the general public welfare, but because they form so central a part of an individual's life. . . .

Only the most willful blindness could obscure the fact that sexual intimacy is "a sensitive, key relationship of human existence, central to family life, community welfare, and the development of human personality." *Paris Adult Theatre I v. Slaton* (1973). The fact that individuals define themselves in a significant way through their intimate sexual relationships with others suggests, in a Nation as diverse as ours, that there may be many "right" ways of conducting those relationships, and that much of the richness of a relationship will come from the freedom an individual has to choose the form and nature of these intensely personal bonds.

In a variety of circumstances we have recognized that a necessary corollary of giving individuals freedom to choose how to conduct their lives is acceptance of the fact that different individuals will make different choices. For example, in holding that the clearly important state interest in public education should give way to a competing claim by the Amish to the effect that extended formal schooling threatened their way of life, the Court declared: "There can be no assumption that today's majority is 'right' and the Amish and others like them are 'wrong.' A way of life that is odd or even erratic but interferes with no rights or interests of others is not to be condemned because it is different." *Wisconsin v. Yoder* (1972). The Court claims that its decision today merely refuses to recognize a fundamental right to engage in homosexual sodomy; what the Court really has refused to recognize is the fundamental interest all individuals have in controlling the nature of their intimate associations with others. . . .

An Unjustifiable Law

The Court's failure to comprehend the magnitude of the liberty interests at stake in this case leads it to slight the question whether petitioner, on behalf of the State, has justified Georgia's infringement on these interests. I believe that neither of the two general justifications for 16-6-2 that petitioner has advanced warrants dismissing respondent's challenge for failure to state a claim.

First, petitioner asserts that the acts made criminal by the statute may have serious adverse consequences for "the general public health and welfare," such as spreading communicable diseases or fostering other criminal activity. Inasmuch as this case was dismissed by the District Court on the pleading, it is not surprising that the record before us is barren of any evidence to support petitioner's claim. . . .

The core of petitioner's defense of 16-6-2, however, is that respondent and others who engage in the conduct prohibited by 16-6-2 interfere with Georgia's exercise of the "'right of the Nation and of the States to maintain a decent society.'" *Paris Adult Theatre I v. Slaton* quoting *Jacobollis v. Ohio* (1964). . . .

The assertion that "traditional Judeo-Christian values proscribe" the conduct involved cannot provide an adequate justification for 16-6-2. That certain, but by no means all, religious groups condemn the behavior at issue gives the State no license to impose their judgments on the entire citizenry. The legitimacy of secular legislation depends instead on whether the State can advance some justification for its law beyond its conformity to religious doctrine. . . .

Nor can 16-6-2 be justified as a "morally neutral" exercise of Georgia's power to "protect the public environment," *Paris Adult Theatre I*. Certainly, some private behavior can affect the fabric of society as a whole. Reasonable people may differ about whether particular sexual acts are moral or immoral, but "we have ample evidence for believing that people will not abandon morality, will not think any better of murder, cruelty and dishonesty, merely because some private sexual practice which they abominate is not punished by the law." H.L.A. Hart, *Immorality and Treason*. . . .

It took but three years for the Court to see the error in its analysis in *Minersville School District v. Gobitis* (1940), and to recognize that the threat to national cohesion posed by a refusal to salute the flag was vastly outweighed by the threat to those same values posed by compelling such a salute. I can only hope that here, too, the Court soon will reconsider its analysis and conclude that depriving individuals of the right to choose for themselves how to conduct their intimate relationships poses a far greater threat to the values most deeply rooted in our Nation's history than tolerance of nonconformity could ever do. Because I think the Court today betrays those values, I dissent.

"People realized that the only way to avoid such outcomes in the future would be to elect new leaders who would appoint new justices."

Bowers Actually Cost the Victor More than the Loser

Laura Douglas-Brown

As Laura Douglas-Brown notes in the following viewpoint, the Bowers *decision came as a shock to the gay community, but fifteen years later the decision may actually have proved more beneficial than harmful. What began as a simple citation for public drinking had escalated into an arrest for sodomy, and many gay people believed the U.S. Supreme Court would be as outraged as they were by the actions of the police and by Georgia's antisodomy statute itself. When the Court found in favor of the prosecution, the decision spurred gay people throughout the country to organize on behalf of overturning sodomy laws and to become more politically active overall. In an ironic twist, Attorney General Michael Bowers was later discovered to have had an extramarital affair and to have thus violated another rarely enforced Georgia statute, the law against adultery, thus ending his political career.*

Laura Douglas-Brown is a longtime lesbian activist and the editor of Southern Voice, *a gay-community newspaper based in Atlanta, Georgia.*

Laura Douglas-Brown, *"Bowers v. Hardwick* at 15," *Southern Voice*, July 12, 2001. Copyright © 2001 A Window Media LLC Publication. Reproduced by permission.

"To hold that the act of homosexual sodomy is somehow protected as a fundamental right would be to cast aside millennia of moral teaching."

The narrow 5–4 decision, in the case of a gay Atlanta man arrested in his own bedroom, sparked immediate outrage: Three days after the July 30, 1986, ruling, more than 200 protesters gathered at Atlanta's Richard B. Russell federal building to denounce the decision.

At the time, 24 states still had sodomy laws on the books: 19, including Georgia's, were broad prohibitions against anal and oral intercourse, while five forbade homosexual acts specifically.

Today [in 2001], 13 states have sodomy laws, and only three of the gay-specific statutes still stand, according to the Lambda Legal Defense & Education Fund. And although Georgia's sodomy law was overturned by the state Supreme Court in 1998, activists and attorneys say the stridently worded ruling in *Bowers v. Hardwick* continues to have impact, both in court cases around the country and in the activists it helped inspire here in Atlanta.

"The *Hardwick* decision continues to say that who you are, in many states, is a felony, and that's a big deal," said attorney Kathleen Wilde, who represented gay Atlanta bartender Michael Hardwick throughout his challenge to the law. "People are scared, and that keeps people in the closet and afraid to come out."

The Two Protagonists

Michael Bowers, the Georgia Attorney General who defended the law, reportedly once said his only regret is that his name did not appear second on the case, "because then it wouldn't look like I'm the homosexual."

Now an attorney with the Atlanta firm Meadows, Ichter & Trigg, Bowers said [in 2001 that] the infamous case "is just not something I think about now."

Asked to discuss his thoughts about the case 15 years after the decision, Bowers declined.

"I'd rather not," he said. "I did my job as best I knew how, and reasonable people can disagree about it, but that's all I want to say about it now."

Michael Hardwick cannot reflect on the case that bears his name: He died in Gainesville, Fla., on June 13, 1991, reportedly from complications from AIDS. His obituary did not mention either his sexual orientation or his role in challenging the sodomy law.

Hardwick "was incredibly courageous," remembered Wilde. "He was quite a warm, wonderful person, and he was an artist, and he became a very articulate speaker for the cause."

Still, the case that would ultimately bring Hardwick into the national spotlight—and legal history—began simply enough. In 1982, Hardwick, a bartender at an Atlanta gay club, left the bar after his shift drinking a beer. He threw it in a trash can, but was cited by police for public drinking.

According to Wilde, the ticket was confusing: It said Wednesday but cited Tuesday's date. When Hardwick missed the court date, a warrant was issued for his arrest. Although Hardwick paid his court fine, the warrant wasn't retracted, and a police officer took the "extraordinary step" of going to his home at 3 a.m. to serve the warrant, Wilde said.

Let into the home by a roommate, the officer entered a bedroom where he saw Hardwick engaged in sodomy with a male partner and arrested him. Fulton County's district attorney declined to prosecute the case, a felony that carried a prison sentence of up to 20 years.

But Hardwick decided to file suit to overturn the law, and many activists thought the case—a man arrested in his own bedroom—offered the perfect opportunity to argue that the law violated privacy rights. The 11th Circuit Court of Appeals agreed, but as Georgia's Attorney General, Bowers appealed to the U.S. Supreme Court and won.

But his vigorous defense of Georgia's sodomy law would also ultimately play a role in ending Bowers' career in public office. In 1998, Bowers resigned as attorney general to seek the Republican nomination for governor. He lost that bid after admitting a long-term extramarital affair—in violation of another of Georgia's archaic sex laws, the law against adultery.

That hypocrisy helped put the nail in the coffin of Bowers' political career, gay political activists said.

"Bowers won the battle, but lost the war," said Harry Knox, executive director of Georgia Equality, the nonpartisan statewide gay political group.

"If anyone wants to say there was a final chapter to [Georgia's sodomy law saga], that may be it—the hypocrisy of Bowers having to admit his indiscretion," agreed longtime gay political lobbyist Larry Pellegrini.

"Afterwards, there was no hero left for those who wanted to restore the sodomy law," he said. "He was their focus, and he was lost."

An Old Development

Gay and lesbian Georgians no longer have to directly contend with the sodomy law, which had been used to justify everything from denying lesbian mothers custody of their children to banning detailed safer sex education.

Twelve years after the *Hardwick* case, in a landmark decision that shocked many gay rights advocates, the Georgia Supreme Court announced that it had struck down the 182-year-old sodomy law as unconstitutional based on the right to privacy guaranteed by the Georgia Constitution. The case involved a heterosexual man convicted of consensual sodomy with his 17-year-old niece. But gay rights activists said the decision's biggest impact would be on gay residents.

"Georgia is now a free state," said Steve Scarborough, staff attorney with Lambda's southern regional office and author of a persuasive "friend of the court" brief in the case.

But while Georgia residents are now "free," the *Hardwick* decision continues to have a "terrible impact across the country," said Harvard Law Professor Laurence H. Tribe, an expert in Constitutional law who argued Hardwick's case before the Supreme Court.

The decision serves "as a ready excuse for much discrimination against gay men, lesbians and bisexuals—especially in matters of employment, family law and immigration—on the ground that individuals who are not heterosexual are by definition inclined to commit acts that remain crimes in many states of the union," Tribe said.

"The power of the excuse that *Bowers v. Hardwick* continues to provide should never be underestimated," Tribe said.

A Legacy of Activism

Still, while the U.S. Supreme Court's decision in *Bowers v. Hardwick* was undeniably negative for gays, "some lingering effects have been positive," according to Pellegrini.

Outrage at the decision helped prompt record numbers of Georgia gays to get involved in political campaigns as voters and volunteers, he said, especially Bill Clinton's 1992 presidential campaign. People realized that the only way to avoid such outcomes in the future would be to elect new leaders who would appoint new justices, Pellegrini said.

In addition to sparking the 1986 protest, the *Hardwick* decision and the sodomy law also played pivotal roles in energizing some of Atlanta's best known gay activists.

Knox, now Georgia Equality's director, said he discussed gay issues publicly for the first time when, as a senior at the University of Georgia in 1984, he gave a presentation in speech class about the then-ongoing *Bowers v. Hardwick* case.

"I felt it was really a denial of my most fundamental being," Knox said.

Pellegrini said he hadn't come out publicly when the Supreme Court ruled in the case in 1986, but his first work lobbying the Georgia General Assembly came in 1991 when he volunteered to collect postcards from around the state from people who supported repealing the sodomy law.

Nearly five years after the *Bowers v. Hardwick* decision, Michael Bowers again took on gay rights issues when in 1991 he withdrew a job offer for lesbian attorney Robin Shahar because of her planned commitment ceremony with her female partner. Bowers cited both *Bowers v. Hardwick* and the sodomy law among his justifications for his actions in a court battle that lasted until 1998, when the U.S. Supreme Court refused to hear Shahar's appeal, allowing an appeals court ruling in favor of Bowers to stand.

But while Bowers' career in government has ended, Shahar's has blossomed. She now serves as senior assistant city attorney for Atlanta, where she works on civil rights cases— including leading the legal fight to approve and implement Atlanta's domestic partner benefits.

CHAPTER 2

Gay People May Not Be Singled Out for Discrimination

Case Overview

Romer v. Evans (1996)

In response to various antidiscrimination statutes in Denver, Aspen, and Boulder, conservatives in Colorado put Amendment 2 on the ballot in 1992. Passed with a majority of 53 percent, the amendment forbade municipalities and school districts from passing or enforcing any legislation that would protect homosexual conduct or relationships or allow gay or bisexual people to claim minority status or any other kind of protected status. Gay rights groups immediately sued for an injunction blocking enforcement of the amendment. Even before the injunction was issued, Colorado's Supreme Court ruled that the state would have to prove that the amendment advanced a "compelling state interest" or it would violate the U.S. Constitution's Fourteenth Amendment's equal protection clause. The state failed to prove this and an injunction was issued. The state appealed, and in 1996 the case reached the U.S. Supreme Court.

The history of Amendment 2 revealed the ambivalence of public opinion on gay rights. By giving gay people protection from discrimination, the elected representatives of Denver and other cities showed that in some places gays were being accepted as a legitimate minority group that had suffered and continue to suffer from bigotry. By striking down those protections, a slight majority of Coloradans showed that they were uncomfortable with the idea of gay rights as simply another phase in the ongoing effort to extend civil rights to all Americans. Along with religious and moral objections, part of the difficulty lay in the idea that gay people were seeking "special rights." One of the arguments that Amendment 2 supporters used was that gay people would start getting special treatment unavailable to the straight majority. It is interesting that the amendment specifically banned quotas for gay people, despite the fact that no municipality had instituted hiring quotas for gays.

In arguing its case, the state of Colorado seized on this very idea, saying that the amendment was really about preventing special rights for homosexuals. In its 6–3 decision, the Supreme Court rejected that argument and in fact claimed the opposite was true. Justice Anthony Kennedy, who wrote the majority opinion, explained that if allowed to stand, the amendment would place a special burden on gay people. Unlike other minority groups seeking the protection of antidiscrimination laws, gay people would not only have to convince a majority of their elected representatives or fellow citizens, they would have to jump through all the hoops designed to make passage of constitutional referendums difficult to pass. Kennedy went on to say that the broad nature of the amendment and the lack of any obvious connection to clear state interests could only be explained by bigotry against gay people, a bigotry that was unacceptable and unconstitutional in government at any level.

In response, Justice Antonin Scalia argued in his dissent that Amendment 2 did not deny the political process to gay people; it simply made it more difficult. Furthermore, in his view, since the Constitution did not specifically defend homosexuality from persecution, the question of the tolerance of homosexuals was left entirely to the democratic process. Prophetically, Scalia also noted that the majority opinion directly contradicted the reasoning in *Bowers v. Hardwick*, setting up a future challenge to that decision. That is precisely what happened in 2003, when the *Lawrence v. Texas* decision overturned *Bowers*.

> *"We must conclude that Amendment 2 classifies homosexuals not to further a proper legislative end but to make them unequal to everyone else."*

The Court's Decision: States Cannot Violate Equal Protection Simply Because They Disapprove of Gays.

Anthony Kennedy

In rejecting Colorado's Amendment 2, which forbade state and local governments from granting any kind of antidiscrimination protection to gay people, Justice Anthony Kennedy explained that such second-class citizenship for a particular group was completely antithetical to the U.S. Constitution. In his view, Colorado had no justification beyond simple dislike for gay people, which was not a legitimate use of government power. He also firmly rejected the theory that Colorado was simply trying to deny "special rights" to gay people, arguing that it was instead creating a special burden for a group of citizens.

Kennedy was appointed to the bench in 1988 by President Ronald Reagan after a career as a constitutional law professor and an appeals court judge. Since then, he has developed a reputation as a key "swing vote" in a number of 5–4 decisions. He also continues to train law students in various seminars.

One century ago, the first Justice [John Marshall] Harlan admonished this Court that the Constitution "neither knows nor tolerates classes among citizens." *Plessy v. Ferguson*

Anthony Kennedy, majority opinion, *Romer v. Evans*, U.S. Supreme Court, 1996.

(1896). Unheeded then, those words now are understood to state a commitment to the law's neutrality where the rights of persons are at stake. The Equal Protection Clause [of the Fourteenth Amendment] enforces this principle and today requires us to hold invalid a provision of Colorado's Constitution.

The enactment challenged in this case is an amendment to the Constitution of the State of Colorado, adopted in a 1992 statewide referendum. The parties and the state courts refer to it as "Amendment 2," its designation when submitted to the voters. The impetus for the amendment and the contentious campaign that preceded its adoption came in large part from ordinances that had been passed in various Colorado municipalities. For example, the cities of Aspen and Boulder and the City and County of Denver each had enacted ordinances which banned discrimination in many transactions and activities, including housing, employment, education, public accommodations, and health and welfare services. What gave rise to the statewide controversy was the protection the ordinances afforded to persons discriminated against by reason of their sexual orientation. . . . Amendment 2 repeals these ordinances to the extent they prohibit discrimination on the basis of "homosexual, lesbian or bisexual orientation, conduct, practices or relationships."

Yet Amendment 2, in explicit terms, does more than repeal or rescind these provisions. It prohibits all legislative, executive or judicial action at any level of state or local government designed to protect the named class, a class we shall refer to as homosexual persons or gays and lesbians. The amendment reads:

> No Protected Status Based on Homosexual, Lesbian, or Bisexual Orientation. Neither the State of Colorado, through any of its branches or departments, nor any of its agencies, political subdivisions, municipalities or school districts, shall enact, adopt or enforce any statute, regulation, ordinance or

policy whereby homosexual, lesbian or bisexual orientation, conduct, practices or relationships shall constitute or otherwise be the basis of or entitle any person or class of persons to have or claim any minority status, quota preferences, protected status or claim of discrimination. This Section of the Constitution shall be in all respects self-executing.

Soon after Amendment 2 was adopted, this litigation to declare its invalidity and enjoin its enforcement was commenced in the District Court for the City and County of Denver. Among the plaintiffs (respondents here) were homosexual persons, some of them government employees. They alleged that enforcement of Amendment 2 would subject them to immediate and substantial risk of discrimination on the basis of their sexual orientation. Other plaintiffs (also respondents here) included the three municipalities whose ordinances we have cited and certain other governmental entities which had acted earlier to protect homosexuals from discrimination but would be prevented by Amendment 2 from continuing to do so. Although Governor [Roy] Romer had been on record opposing the adoption of Amendment 2, he was named in his official capacity as a defendant, together with the Colorado Attorney General and the State of Colorado. . . .

The Objective of Amendment 2

The State's principal argument in defense of Amendment 2 is that it puts gays and lesbians in the same position as all other persons. So, the State says, the measure does no more than deny homosexuals special rights. This reading of the amendment's language is implausible. We rely not upon our own interpretation of the amendment but upon the authoritative construction of Colorado's Supreme Court. The state court, deeming it unnecessary to determine the full extent of the amendment's reach, found it invalid even on a modest reading of its implications. The critical discussion of the amendment, set out in *Evans* I [*Evans v. Romer*, 1993], is as follows:

The immediate objective of Amendment 2 is, at a minimum, to repeal existing statutes, regulations, ordinances, and policies of state and local entities that barred discrimination based on sexual orientation. See Aspen, Colo., Mun. Code 13-98 (1977) (prohibiting discrimination in employment, housing and public accommodations on the basis of sexual orientation).

The "ultimate effect" of Amendment 2 is to prohibit any governmental entity from adopting similar, or more protective statutes, regulations, ordinances, or policies in the future unless the state constitution is first amended to permit such measures.

Sweeping and comprehensive is the change in legal status effected by this law. So much is evident from the ordinances that the Colorado Supreme Court declared would be void by operation of Amendment 2. Homosexuals, by state decree, are put in a solitary class with respect to transactions and relations in both the private and governmental spheres. The amendment withdraws from homosexuals, but no others, specific legal protection from the injuries caused by discrimination, and it forbids reinstatement of these laws and policies.

The change that Amendment 2 works in the legal status of gays and lesbians in the private sphere is far-reaching, both on its own terms and when considered in light of the structure and operation of modern anti-discrimination laws. That structure is well illustrated by contemporary statutes and ordinances prohibiting discrimination by providers of public accommodations. "At common law, innkeepers, smiths, and others who 'made profession of a public employment,' were prohibited from refusing, without good reason, to serve a customer." *Hurley v. Irish-American Gay, Lesbian and Bisexual Group of Boston, Inc.* (1995). The duty was a general one and did not specify protection for particular groups. The common law rules, however, proved insufficient in many instances, and it was settled early that the Fourteenth Amendment did not give Congress a general power to prohibit discrimination in public accommodations. . . .

Colorado's state and municipal laws typify this emerging tradition of statutory protection and follow a consistent pattern. The laws first enumerate the persons or entities subject to a duty not to discriminate. The list goes well beyond the entities covered by the common law. The Boulder ordinance, for example, has a comprehensive definition of entities deemed places of "public accommodation." They include "any place of business engaged in any sales to the general public and any place that offers services, facilities, privileges, or advantages to the general public or that receives financial support through solicitation of the general public or through governmental subsidy of any kind." . . .

Amendment 2 bars homosexuals from securing protection against the injuries that these public-accommodations laws address. That in itself is a severe consequence, but there is more. Amendment 2, in addition, nullifies specific legal protections for this targeted class in all transactions in housing, sale of real estate, insurance, health and welfare services, private education, and employment.

The Amendment Would Rescind Many Protections

Not confined to the private sphere, Amendment 2 also operates to repeal and forbid all laws or policies providing specific protection for gays or lesbians from discrimination by every level of Colorado government. The State Supreme Court cited two examples of protections in the governmental sphere that are now rescinded and may not be reintroduced. The first is Colorado Executive Order D0035 (1990), which forbids employment discrimination against "'all state employees, classified and exempt' on the basis of sexual orientation." Also repealed, and now forbidden, are "various provisions prohibiting discrimination based on sexual orientation at state colleges." The repeal of these measures and the prohibition against their future reenactment demonstrates that Amendment 2 has the same force and effect in Colorado's governmental sector as it does elsewhere and that it applies to policies as well as ordinary legislation.

Amendment 2's reach may not be limited to specific laws passed for the benefit of gays and lesbians. It is a fair, if not necessary, inference from the broad language of the amendment that it deprives gays and lesbians even of the protection of general laws and policies that prohibit arbitrary discrimination in governmental and private settings. . . .

At some point in the systematic administration of these laws, an official must determine whether homosexuality is an arbitrary and thus forbidden basis for decision. Yet a decision to that effect would itself amount to a policy prohibiting discrimination on the basis of homosexuality, and so would appear to be no more valid under Amendment 2 than the specific prohibitions against discrimination the state court held invalid.

If this consequence follows from Amendment 2, as its broad language suggests, it would compound the constitutional difficulties the law creates. The state court did not decide whether the amendment has this effect, however, and neither need we. In the course of rejecting the argument that Amendment 2 is intended to conserve resources to fight discrimination against suspect classes, the Colorado Supreme Court made the limited observation that the amendment is not intended to affect many anti-discrimination laws protecting non-suspect classes. In our view that does not resolve the issue. In any event, even if, as we doubt, homosexuals could find some safe harbor in laws of general application, we cannot accept the view that Amendment 2's prohibition on specific legal protections does no more than deprive homosexuals of special rights. To the contrary, the amendment imposes a special disability upon those persons alone. Homosexuals are forbidden the safeguards that others enjoy or may seek without constraint. They can obtain specific protection against discrimination only by enlisting the citizenry of Colorado to amend the state constitution or perhaps, on the State's view, by trying to pass helpful laws of general applicability. This is so no matter how local or discrete the harm, no matter how public and widespread the injury. We find nothing special in the protections Amendment 2 withholds. These are protections taken for granted by most people either because they already have them or do not need them; these are protections against exclusion from an almost limitless number of transactions and endeavors that constitute ordinary civic life in a free society.

The Fourteenth Amendment's promise that no person shall be denied the equal protection of the laws must co-exist with the practical necessity that most legislation classifies for one purpose or another, with resulting disadvantage to various groups or persons. . . .

Amendment 2 fails, indeed defies, even this conventional inquiry. First, the amendment has the peculiar property of imposing a broad and undifferentiated disability on a single named group, an exceptional and, as we shall explain, invalid form of legislation. Second, its sheer breadth is so discontinuous with the reasons offered for it that the amendment seems inexplicable by anything but animus toward the class that it affects; it lacks a rational relationship to legitimate state interests.

Taking the first point, even in the ordinary equal protection case calling for the most deferential of standards, we insist on knowing the relation between the classification adopted and the object to be attained. The search for the link between classification and objective gives substance to the Equal Protection Clause; it provides guidance and discipline for the legislature, which is entitled to know what sorts of laws it can pass; and it marks the limits of our own authority. In the ordinary case, a law will be sustained if it can be said to advance a legitimate government interest, even if the law seems unwise or works to the disadvantage of a particular group, or if the rationale for it seems tenuous. . . .

Amendment 2 confounds this normal process of judicial review. It is at once too narrow and too broad. It identifies persons by a single trait and then denies them protection across the board. The resulting disqualification of a class of persons from the right to seek specific protection from the law is unprecedented in our jurisprudence.

Violation of Equal Protection

It is not within our constitutional tradition to enact laws of this sort. Central both to the idea of the rule of law and to our own Constitution's guarantee of equal protection is the principle that government and each of its parts remain open on impartial terms to all who seek its assistance. . . . Respect for this principle explains why laws singling out a certain class of citizens for disfavored legal status or general hardships are rare. A law declaring that in general it shall be more difficult for one group of citizens than for all others to seek aid from the government is itself a denial of equal protection of the laws in the most literal sense. . . .

A second and related point is that laws of the kind now before us raise the inevitable inference that the disadvantage imposed is born of animosity toward the class of persons affected. "[I]f the constitutional conception of 'equal protection of the laws' means anything, it must at the very least mean that a bare . . . desire to harm a politically unpopular group cannot constitute a legitimate governmental interest." *Department of Agriculture v. Moreno* (1973). Even laws enacted for broad and ambitious purposes often can be explained by reference to legitimate public policies which justify the incidental disadvantages they impose on certain persons. Amendment 2, however, in making a general announcement that gays and lesbians shall not have any particular protections from the law, inflicts on them immediate, continuing, and real injuries that outrun and belie any legitimate justifications that may be claimed for it. We conclude that, in addition to the far-reaching deficiencies of Amendment 2 that we have noted, the principles it offends, in another sense, are conventional and venerable; a law must bear a rational relationship to a legitimate governmental purpose and Amendment 2 does not.

The primary rationale the State offers for Amendment 2 is respect for other citizens' freedom of association, and in particular the liberties of landlords or employers who have personal or religious objections to homosexuality. Colorado also cites its interest in conserving resources to fight discrimination against other groups. The breadth of the Amendment is so far removed from these particular justifications that we find it impossible to credit them. We cannot say that Amendment 2 is directed to any identifiable legitimate purpose or discrete objective. It is a status-based enactment divorced from any factual context from which we could discern a relationship to legitimate state interests; it is a classification of persons undertaken for its own sake, something the Equal Protection Clause does not permit. "[C]lass legislation . . . [is] obnoxious to the prohibitions of the Fourteenth Amendment. . . ." Civil Rights Cases, 109 U.S., at 24.

We must conclude that Amendment 2 classifies homosexuals not to further a proper legislative end but to make them unequal to everyone else. This Colorado cannot do. A State cannot so deem a class of persons a stranger to its laws. Amendment 2 violates the Equal Protection Clause, and the judgment of the Supreme Court of Colorado is affirmed.

> *"In holding that homosexuality cannot be singled out for disfavorable treatment, the Court . . . places the prestige of the institution behind the proposition that opposition to homosexuality is as reprehensible as racial or religious bias."*

Dissenting Opinion: The Court Is Substituting Its Own Elitist Views for the Will of the People.

Antonin Scalia

In a sharply worded dissent in Romer v. Evans, *Justice Antonin Scalia, joined by Justice Clarence Thomas and Chief Justice William Rehnquist, accused the Court of ignoring the clear intent of Colorado's Amendment 2. For him, the law simply refused to grant special rights to homosexuals and the Court was unjustified in finding that it imposed any special burden on gay people. Rather than protecting an oppressed minority group, Scalia argues, the Court was in fact granting special protection to a group favored by political and legal elites, the very elites that tend to make up the majority of judges. He also condemned the majority for ignoring the precedent it had established in* Bowers v. Hardwick *just ten years before that denied any fundamental right to homosexual conduct and gave states the sole right to regulate homosexuality.*

Antonin Scalia, dissenting opinion, *Romer v. Evans*, U.S. Supreme Court, 1996.

After a career in private practice and academia, Antonin Scalia entered public service in the Richard Nixon administration, and then served as an assistant attorney general for President Gerald Ford. In 1986, President Ronald Reagan appointed him to the Supreme Court, where he has emerged as a forceful and articulate leader of the Court's conservative wing.

The Court has mistaken a Kulturkampf[1] for a fit of spite. The constitutional amendment before us here is not the manifestation of a "'bare ... desire to harm'" homosexuals, but is rather a modest attempt by seemingly tolerant Coloradans to preserve traditional sexual mores against the efforts of a politically powerful minority to revise those mores through use of the laws. That objective, and the means chosen to achieve it, are not only unimpeachable under any constitutional doctrine hitherto pronounced (hence the opinion's heavy reliance upon principles of righteousness rather than judicial holdings); they have been specifically approved by the Congress of the United States and by this Court.

In holding that homosexuality cannot be singled out for disfavorable treatment, the Court contradicts a decision, unchallenged here, pronounced only 10 years ago, see *Bowers v. Hardwick* (1986), and places the prestige of this institution behind the proposition that opposition to homosexuality is as reprehensible as racial or religious bias. Whether it is or not is precisely the cultural debate that gave rise to the Colorado constitutional amendment (and to the preferential laws against which the amendment was directed). Since the Constitution of the United States says nothing about this subject, it is left to be resolved by normal democratic means, including the democratic adoption of provisions in state constitutions. This Court has no business imposing upon all Americans the resolution favored by the elite class from which the Members of

---

1. Literally, a "culture struggle," as in a society's decision to embrace or reject traditional sexual mores.

this institution are selected, pronouncing that "animosity" to-ward homosexuality, is evil. I vigorously dissent.

Discrimination Still Illegal Under Amendment

Let me first discuss Part II of the Court's opinion, its longest section, which is devoted to rejecting the State's arguments that Amendment 2 "puts gays and lesbians in the same posi-tion as all other persons," and "does no more than deny ho-mosexuals special rights." The Court concludes that this read-ing of Amendment 2's language is "implausible" under the "authoritative construction" given Amendment 2 by the Su-preme Court of Colorado.

In reaching this conclusion, the Court considers it unnec-essary to decide the validity of the State's argument that Amendment 2 does not deprive homosexuals of the "protec-tion [afforded by] general laws and policies that prohibit arbi-trary discrimination in governmental and private settings." I agree that we need not resolve that dispute, because the Su-preme Court of Colorado has resolved it for us. In *Evans v. Romer* (1994), the Colorado court stated:

> "[I]t is significant to note that Colorado law currently pro-scribes discrimination against persons who are not suspect classes, including discrimination based on age, marital or family status, veterans' status, and for any legal, off-duty conduct such as smoking tobacco. Of course Amendment 2 is not intended to have any effect on this legislation, but seeks only to prevent the adoption of anti-discrimination laws intended to protect gays, lesbians, and bisexuals."

The Court utterly fails to distinguish this portion of the Colorado court's opinion. Colorado Rev. Stat. (1995), which this passage authoritatively declares not to be affected by Amendment 2, was respondents' primary example of a gener-ally applicable law whose protections would be unavailable to homosexuals under Amendment 2. The clear import of the

Colorado court's conclusion that it is not affected is that "general laws and policies that prohibit arbitrary discrimination" would continue to prohibit discrimination on the basis of homosexual conduct as well. This analysis, which is fully in accord with (indeed, follows inescapably from) the text of the constitutional provision, lays to rest such horribles, raised in the course of oral argument, as the prospect that assaults upon homosexuals could not be prosecuted. The amendment prohibits special treatment of homosexuals, and nothing more. It would not affect, for example, a requirement of state law that pensions be paid to all retiring state employees with a certain length of service; homosexual employees, as well as others, would be entitled to that benefit. But it would prevent the State or any municipality from making death-benefit payments to the "life partner" of a homosexual when it does not make such payments to the long-time roommate of a nonhomosexual employee. Or again, it does not affect the requirement of the State's general insurance laws that customers be afforded coverage without discrimination unrelated to anticipated risk. Thus, homosexuals could not be denied coverage, or charged a greater premium, with respect to auto collision insurance; but neither the State nor any municipality could require that distinctive health insurance risks associated with homosexuality (if there are any) be ignored.

The Question of Equal Protection

Despite all of its hand-wringing about the potential effect of Amendment 2 on general antidiscrimination laws, the Court's opinion ultimately does not dispute all this, but assumes it to be true. The only denial of equal treatment it contends homosexuals have suffered is this: They may not obtain preferential treatment without amending the state constitution. That is to say, the principle underlying the Court's opinion is that one who is accorded equal treatment under the laws, but cannot as readily as others obtain preferential treatment under the laws, has been denied equal protection of the laws. If merely stating this alleged "equal protection" violation does not suffice to refute it, our constitutional jurisprudence has achieved terminal silliness.

The central thesis of the Court's reasoning is that any group is denied equal protection when, to obtain advantage (or, presumably, to avoid disadvantage), it must have recourse to a more general and hence more difficult level of political decisionmaking than others. The world has never heard of such a principle, which is why the Court's opinion is so long on emotive utterance and so short on relevant legal citation. And it seems to me most unlikely that any multilevel democracy can function under such a principle. For whenever a disadvantage is imposed, or conferral of a benefit is prohibited, at one of the higher levels of democratic decisionmaking (i.e., by the state legislature rather than local government, or by the people at large in the state constitution rather than the legislature), the affected group has (under this theory) been denied equal protection. To take the simplest of examples, consider a state law prohibiting the award of municipal contracts to relatives of mayors or city councilmen. Once such a law is passed, the group composed of such relatives must, in order to get the benefit of city contracts, persuade the state legislature—unlike all other citizens, who need only persuade the municipality. It is ridiculous to consider this a denial of equal protection, which is why the Court's theory is unheard-of. . . .

Upholding *Bowers*

I turn next to whether there was a legitimate rational basis for the substance of the constitutional amendment—for the prohibition of special protection for homosexuals. It is unsurprising that the Court avoids discussion of this question, since the answer is so obviously yes. The case most relevant to the issue before us today is not even mentioned in the Court's opinion:

In *Bowers v. Hardwick* (1986), we held that the Constitution does not prohibit what virtually all States had done from the founding of the Republic until very recent years—making homosexual conduct a crime. That holding is unassailable, except by those who think that the Constitution changes to suit current fashions. But in any event it is a given in the present case: Respondents' briefs did not urge overruling *Bowers,* and at oral argument respondents' counsel expressly disavowed any intent to seek such overruling. If it is constitutionally permissible for a State to make homosexual conduct criminal, surely it is constitutionally permissible for a State to enact other laws merely disfavoring homosexual conduct. . . .

But assuming that, in Amendment 2, a person of homosexual "orientation" is someone who does not engage in homosexual conduct but merely has a tendency or desire to do so, *Bowers* still suffices to establish a rational basis for the provision. If it is rational to criminalize the conduct, surely it is rational to deny special favor and protection to those with a self-avowed tendency or desire to engage in the conduct. Indeed, where criminal sanctions are not involved, homosexual "orientation" is an acceptable stand-in for homosexual conduct. A State "does not violate the Equal Protection Clause merely because the classifications made by its laws are imperfect." *Dandridge v. Williams* (1970). . . .

Colorado, Unlike the Court, Is Being Reasonable

The foregoing suffices to establish what the Court's failure to cite any case remotely in point would lead one to suspect: No principle set forth in the Constitution, nor even any imagined by this Court in the past 200 years, prohibits what Colorado has done here. But the case for Colorado is much stronger than that. What it has done is not only unprohibited, but eminently reasonable, with close, congressionally approved precedent in earlier constitutional practice.

First, as to its eminent reasonableness. The Court's opinion contains grim, disapproving hints that Coloradans have been guilty of "animus" or "animosity" toward homosexuality, as though that has been established as Unamerican. Of course it is our moral heritage that one should not hate any human being or class of human beings. But I had thought that one could consider certain conduct reprehensible—murder, for example, or polygamy, or cruelty to animals—and could exhibit even "animus" toward such conduct. Surely that is the only sort of "animus" at issue here: moral disapproval of homosexual conduct, the same sort of moral disapproval that produced the centuries-old criminal laws that we held constitutional in *Bowers*. The Colorado amendment does not, to speak entirely precisely, prohibit giving favored status to people who are homosexuals; they can be favored for many reasons—for example, because they are senior citizens or members of racial minorities. But it prohibits giving them favored status because of their homosexual conduct—that is, it prohibits favored status for homosexuality.

But though Coloradans are, as I say, entitled to be hostile toward homosexual conduct, the fact is that the degree of hostility reflected by Amendment 2 is the smallest conceivable. The Court's portrayal of Coloradans as a society fallen victim to pointless, hate-filled "gay-bashing" is so false as to be comical. Colorado not only is one of the 25 States that have repealed their antisodomy laws, but was among the first to do so. But the society that eliminates criminal punishment for homosexual acts does not necessarily abandon the view that homosexuality is morally wrong and socially harmful; often, abolition simply reflects the view that enforcement of such criminal laws involves unseemly intrusion into the intimate lives of citizens.

There is a problem, however, which arises when criminal sanction of homosexuality is eliminated but moral and social disapprobation of homosexuality is meant to be retained. The

Court cannot be unaware of that problem; it is evident in many cities of the country, and occasionally bubbles to the surface of the news, in heated political disputes over such matters as the introduction into local schools of books teaching that homosexuality is an optional and fully acceptable "alternate life style." The problem (a problem, that is, for those who wish to retain social disapprobation of homosexuality) is that, because those who engage in homosexual conduct tend to reside in disproportionate numbers in certain communities, and of course care about homosexual-rights issues much more ardently than the public at large, they possess political power much greater than their numbers, both locally and statewide. Quite understandably, they devote this political power to achieving not merely a grudging social toleration, but full social acceptance, of homosexuality.

Right to Oppose Social Acceptance

By the time Coloradans were asked to vote on Amendment 2, their exposure to homosexuals' quest for social endorsement was not limited to newspaper accounts of happenings in places such as New York, Los Angeles, San Francisco, and Key West [Florida]. Three Colorado cities—Aspen, Boulder, and Denver had enacted ordinances that listed "sexual orientation" as an impermissible ground for discrimination, equating the moral disapproval of homosexual conduct with racial and religious bigotry. The phenomenon had even appeared statewide: the Governor of Colorado had signed an executive order pronouncing that "in the State of Colorado we recognize the diversity in our pluralistic society and strive to bring an end to discrimination in any form," and directing state agency-heads to "ensure non-discrimination" in hiring and promotion based on, among other things, "sexual orientation." I do not mean to be critical of these legislative successes; homosexuals are as entitled to use the legal system for reinforcement of their moral sentiments as are the rest of society. But they are subject to being countered by lawful, democratic countermeasures as well.

That is where Amendment 2 came in. It sought to counter both the geographic concentration and the disproportionate political power of homosexuals by (1) resolving the controversy at the statewide level, and (2) making the election a single-issue contest for both sides. It put directly, to all the citizens of the State, the question: Should homosexuality be given special protection? They answered no. The Court today asserts that this most democratic of procedures is unconstitutional. Lacking any cases to establish that facially absurd proposition, it simply asserts that it must be unconstitutional, because it has never happened before.

Courts Should Stay Neutral in Culture Wars

I would not myself indulge in . . . official praise for heterosexual monogamy, because I think it no business of the courts (as opposed the political branches) to take sides in this culture war.

But the Court today has done so, not only by inventing a novel and extravagant constitutional doctrine to take the victory away from traditional forces, but even by verbally disparaging as bigotry adherence to traditional attitudes. To suggest, for example, that this constitutional amendment springs from nothing more than "'a bare . . . desire to harm a politically unpopular group,'" quoting *Department of Agriculture v. Moreno* (1973), is nothing short of insulting. (It is also nothing short of preposterous to call "politically unpopular" a group which enjoys enormous influence in American media and politics, and which, as the trial court here noted, though composing no more than 4% of the population had the support of 46% of the voters on Amendment 2.)

When the Court takes sides in the culture wars, it tends to be with the knights rather than the villains—and more specifically with the Templars, reflecting the views and values of the lawyer class from which the Court's Members are drawn. How that class feels about homosexuality will be evident to anyone who wishes to interview job applicants at virtually any of the Nation's law schools. The interviewer may refuse to offer a job because the applicant is a Republican; because he is an adulterer; because he went to the wrong prep school or belongs to the wrong country club; because he eats snails; because he is a womanizer; because she wears real-animal fur; or even because he hates the Chicago Cubs. But if the interviewer should wish not to be an associate or partner of an applicant because he disapproves of the applicant's homosexuality, then he will have violated the pledge which the Association of American Law Schools requires all its member-schools to exact from job interviewers: "assurance of the employer's willingness" to hire homosexuals. This law-school view of what "prejudices" must be stamped out may be contrasted with the more plebeian attitudes that apparently still prevail in the United States Congress, which has been unresponsive to repeated attempts to extend to homosexuals the protections of federal civil rights laws. . . .

Today's opinion has no foundation in American constitutional law, and barely pretends to. The people of Colorado have adopted an entirely reasonable provision which does not even disfavor homosexuals in any substantive sense, but merely denies them preferential treatment. Amendment 2 is designed to prevent piecemeal deterioration of the sexual morality favored by a majority of Coloradans, and is not only an appropriate means to that legitimate end, but a means that Americans have employed before. Striking it down is an act, not of judicial judgment, but of political will. I dissent.

| "Striking down Amendment 2 as entirely
irrational would be a very aggressive
position for a judge to take."

Striking Down Amendment 2 Is Not Justified

Jeffrey Rosen

Shortly before the Romer v. Evans *decision, Jeffrey Rosen, a law professor at the George Washington University and the legal affairs editor for the* New Republic, *considered the merits of the case. He questions the wisdom and justice of Amendment 2, which forbade any governmental entity in Colorado from providing specific protections for gay people. However, Rosen finds that the state could justify the amendment on the narrow grounds that it would prevent so-called special rights for homosexuals, although it would still be barred from arbitrary actions against them. In addition, he rejects the argument that Amendment 2 would deny gay people equal political participation rights as hopelessly flawed, because it seems to be based on the idea that the people themselves, voting for an amendment to the state constitution, are somehow less legitimate than the people's representatives acting as a state legislature.*

Rosen is a frequent television commentator on legal matters and is the author of The Most Democratic Branch: How the Courts Serve America.

Two years ago [in 1993] in a Denver courtroom, when we last encountered the anti-gay rights case *Evans v. Romer*, Professors Martha Nussbaum of Brown and Robert George of

Jeffrey Rosen, "Disoriented," *The New Republic*, vol. 213, October 23, 1995, pp. 24-26. Copyright © 1995 by The New Republic, Inc. Reproduced by permission of *The New Republic*.

Princeton were wrangling about the proper translation of *tolmema*, Plato's adjective for homosexuality. Nussbaum said "deed of daring"; George preferred "abomination." ... In its journey up to the Supreme Court, however, the case has been transformed from one about the definition of homosexuality to one about constitutional limitations on plebiscitary democracy [direct democracy through citizens' votes]. State and federal courts in Colorado and Ohio, in striking down anti-gay rights initiatives, have come close to suggesting that direct democracy is itself unconstitutional. If the Supreme Court agrees, then the wave of ballot initiatives sweeping across the Western states, including the anti-affirmative action referendums that are pending in California and Washington, could be stopped cold.

But the Supreme Court is unlikely to agree. The notion that anti-gay rights initiatives violate the "fundamental right to political participation" of gay voters, as the Colorado court held, is nebulous and unconvincing, and the justices will almost certainly reject it. There are more modest arguments for striking down the initiative—it's irrational, perhaps, for Colorado to deny civil rights protections to homosexuals that are extended to virtually every other group of citizens, including married people, veterans and smokers. But none of these arguments is entirely persuasive. I'd gladly vote against the anti-gay rights initiative as a citizen of Colorado, but that's not the same as saying it's unconstitutional. Indeed, if the initiative is construed narrowly rather than broadly, the Court probably should, and probably will, uphold it.

In November, 1992, 53 percent of the voters of Colorado ratified Amendment 2 to the Colorado Constitution:

NO PROTECTED STATUS BASED ON HOMOSEXUAL, LESBIAN, OR BISEXUAL ORIENTATION. Neither the State of Colorado, through any of its branches or departments, nor any of its agencies, political subdivisions, municipalities or school districts, shall enact, adopt or enforce any statute, regulation, ordinance or policy whereby homosexual, lesbian or bisexual orientation, conduct, practices or relationships shall constitute or otherwise be the basis of, or entitle any person or class of persons to have, or claim any minority status, quota preferences, protected status or claim of discrimination.

What, exactly, does this tortuous sentence mean? If you read it as expansively as possible, the last phrase of the Amendment, prohibiting "claims of discrimination" on the basis of homosexual orientation, could sweep away all efforts by state government to protect gay people from private and public discrimination, including police regulations requiring equal enforcement of the criminal laws; protections against arbitrary dismissal of state employees; state university non-discrimination policies; state regulations of the insurance industry, and so on. But, read as narrowly as possible, the Amendment might have few practical effects because homosexuals may already be protected by generic laws forbidding discrimination on the basis of factors unrelated to the task at hand. Amendment 2, on this reading, may be nothing more than a refusal by the state to affirm the legitimacy of homosexuality as such. Which of these two readings is correct is the critical—and almost impenetrable—issue in the case.

Equal Rights and Special Rights

"Equal rights, not special rights," proclaimed Amendment 2 bumper stickers; but the *Romer* case shows that it's not easy to distinguish equal rights from special rights in an age when anti-discrimination laws are the norm rather than the exception. In his ... book, *Virtually Normal,* Andrew Sullivan argues that "all public (as opposed to private) discrimination against homosexuals be ended." Sullivan would ban "all proactive discrimination by the state against homosexuals," including discrimination by police officers, government agencies, the military and marriage bureaus, but he opposes civil rights protections for gays in the "private sphere," and he would permit private employers and landlords to discriminate against or in favor of homosexuals as they pleased.

Sullivan's classically liberal distinction between public and private discrimination is conceptually pure; but, as the messy reality of Colorado shows, it has been largely overtaken by the rights revolutions of the post–New Deal administrative state. If we lived in John Stuart Mill's England, where private employers were free to fire their employees at will, it would be easy to applaud Amendment 2 for ensuring that homosexuals have the same protections every other group has against being fired without good reason—namely, no protection at all.

But Colorado in 1995 looks nothing like Colorado in 1895. The private sector is now so pervasively regulated that private employers and landlords are treated more like public utilities than like mom-and-pop proprietors; and the libertarian ideal of freedom of contract has been largely repudiated. In 1990, after heavy lobbying by the tobacco industry, Colorado adopted a "Smoker's Bill of Rights" which prohibits private employers from discriminating against their employees on the basis of any legal off-duty conduct. Sodomy, like smoking, is legal in Colorado. And in many cases, homosexuality is simply defined as the propensity or habit of practicing sodomy. In other words, the civil rights laws of Colorado today appear to protect all citizens from irrational public and private discrimination. If protection against arbitrary discrimination is indeed the baseline of equal rights, rather than special rights, in Colorado (and this is open to question) then singling out homosexuals as uniquely unprotected by the web of protections that everyone else enjoys might plausibly be seen as a denial of the equal protection of the laws.

The proliferation of protected groups in Colorado also makes it harder to argue that anti-discrimination protections are a kind of special rights rather than equal rights. Private employers in Colorado are generally forbidden from discriminating not only on the basis of race, sex and religion, but also on the basis of disability, marital status, political affiliation and veteran status, as well as, in some cities, sexual orientation. As Judge Richard Posner asks in *Sex and Reason*:

> [I]s there any reason to exclude homosexuals from a protected category that already includes not only racial, religious, and ethnic groups but also women, the physically and mentally handicapped, all workers aged 40 and older, and, in some cases, even young healthy male WASPs [white Anglo-Saxon Protestants]? Is there less, or less harmful, or less irrational discrimination against homosexuals than against the members of any of these other groups? The answer is no.

Judicial Restraint

Nevertheless, striking down Amendment 2 as entirely irrational would be a very aggressive position for a judge to take: few citizens really believe that classifications based on sexual orientation are, in all circumstances, entirely unreasonable. In the spirit of judicial restraint, therefore, it might be possible to read the Amendment in a way that minimizes the constitutional difficulties, rather than exaggerating them. At the trial and in its briefs, the state of Colorado went out of its way to insist that firing a state employee because she was gay would indeed be arbitrary and illegal under current state and federal law. The point of Amendment 2, they insisted, was to prevent the state from passing special laws that said so explicitly. So perhaps the Amendment could be construed to forbid the state from passing laws that explicitly forbid discrimination on the basis of homosexual orientation; but not to prevent gays and lesbians from invoking neutral laws, like the Smoker's Bill of Rights, that prohibit arbitrary discrimination against all citizens.

This is a generous reading of a sloppily drafted Amendment; but it may capture something of the conflicted impulses of the more moderate supporters of Amendment 2, who claimed to oppose discrimination against homosexuals and, in the same breath, also claimed to oppose state laws that go out of their way to prohibit discrimination against gays. And perhaps the conflicted impulses aren't entirely illogical. The law, for better or worse, has an expressive dimension; and by adding sexual orientation to a list of less morally controversial characteristics, such as race and gender, some citizens may fear that the state is officially endorsing emotions and conduct that they would rather it didn't. In some ways, Amendment 2 is a civil, statewide version of "Don't Ask Don't Tell." It recognizes that homosexuals exist, even tolerates their private lives, but refuses to grant them any public recognition as equal citizens. Amendment 2 reflects the fact that many heterosexuals seem perfectly willing to extend equal rights to gay men and lesbians, as long as the rights aren't demanded too obviously. It's the anti-discrimination law that dare not speak its name.

Political Participation Argument

Unfortunately, the central question in the Colorado case—what is the baseline for distinguishing equal rights and special rights?—may never be engaged by the Rehnquist Court, thanks to a baffling opinion by the Supreme Court of Colorado. The Colorado Supreme Court struck down Amendment 2, reaffirming its earlier holding that "[t]he right to participate equally in the political process is clearly affected by Amendment 2, because it bars gay men, lesbians, and bisexuals from having an effective voice in governmental affairs."

The weaknesses of this theory are obvious enough. The class of people affected by Amendment 2 is not all gay men, lesbians and bisexuals, but instead all citizens—gay and straight—who happen to support laws that prohibit discrimination on the basis of sexual orientation. And it is hard to see how this group, defined by its political views rather than its sexual orientation, is barred from participating in the political process. As the state of Colorado argues in its brief, no citizens have been disenfranchised, prevented from casting an equally weighted vote, or in any way hindered in electing the representative of their choice.

Of course, Colorado voters who support anti-discrimination protections for gays and lesbians must now seek change through constitutional politics, rather than ordinary politics. But no one has a right to have certain issues decided by representatives of the people rather than the people themselves. In its starkest form, the political participation argument evokes the most radical arguments of [Harvard law professor] Lani Guinier, who suggested that competing groups of citizens are proportionately entitled to have their substantive political agendas actually enacted by legislatures, at least some of the time.

Stripped of its legalisms, the political participation argument is really an argument against plebiscitary democracy. Quoting James Madison on the dangers of majority factionalism, Julian Eule of UCLA argues that all of the filtering mechanisms present in ordinary legislative decisions—informed deliberation, political horsetrading, coalition building, and so forth—are dangerously absent in the crude, one-shot majoritarianism of a constitutional referendum. But this is a utopian view of the way legislatures operate. It's hard to argue with a straight face that the debate in Congress about, for example, the balanced budget amendment was more deliberate and soberly Madisonian than the debate among the citizens of Colorado about Amendment 2. Morever, the anti-populists are quoting Madison out of context; the constitutional guarantee of a Republican Form of Government, far from expressing a suspicion of direct democracy, was in fact designed to protect the right of a majority of citizens to alter and abolish their governments as they pleased.

Equal Protection Argument

More convincing arguments are available, and the best of them appears in an exceptional brief filed by [Harvard law professor] Laurence Tribe. Avoiding flamboyant claims about political participation, Tribe argues that Amendment 2 is a literal violation of the Equal Protection Clause of the Fourteenth Amendment, which says that "[n]o state shall . . . deny to any person within its jurisdiction the equal protection of the laws." By creating, for homosexuals, "a unique hole in the state's fabric of existing and potential legal protections" against the wrong of "discrimination," Tribe argues, Colorado has provided "a paradigm case of what it means for a state to structure its legal system so as to 'deny' to 'person[s] within its jurisdiction the equal protection of the laws.'"

When it comes to the administration and enforcement of existing state laws, Tribe is clearly right that gay men and lesbians in Colorado, in the wake of Amendment 2, have less protection than the most favored classes of citizens. For example, imagine that the police decided not to prosecute murderers in Colorado when the victims were homosexual. Homosexuals would, indeed, be prohibited by Amendment 2 from invoking the Denver police department regulation which provides that "Members [must] be of service to anyone . . . in danger . . . regardless of race, . . . gender, age or sexual orientation." But this wouldn't leave homosexuals any worse off than, say, left-handed people, who don't have the benefit of special police department regulations or executive orders prohibiting state officers from discriminating against them in the first place. (Left-handed people, however, arguably need special regulations less than homosexuals do.) And of course, homosexuals and left-handed people and everyone else continue to be protected by the federal Constitution, which protects all persons, regardless of their status, from arbitrary and irrational state actions.

The weakness of Tribe's elegant argument is that it relies on an unusually abstract definition of "discrimination." Tribe concedes that the Colorado Legislature has no obligation to adopt laws protecting homosexuals from private discrimination in housing or employment, making a distinction that puts him in uneasy agreement with Sullivan. He also concedes that if the Colorado Legislature did adopt civil rights protections for homosexuals, it would be free to change its mind and to repeal them. But he argues that the citizens of Colorado, in a popular referendum, should not be permitted to preclude homosexuals from receiving even the possibility of future protection under any state or local law from an entire category of injurious conduct at least some of which is "concededly wrongful." This is the point where Tribe's argument seems to break down. After all, firing a gay employee, or refusing to rent a house to a gay tenant, is not "concededly wrongful" in a state like Colorado that has declined to adopt laws banning employment or housing discrimination on the basis of sexual orientation. By defining the wrong of "discrimination" so abstractly, Tribe elides the difference between forms of discrimination that are and are not wrongful and illegal under state and federal law. Tribe is right that some of the discrimination that Amendment 2 insulates from challenge is "concededly wrongful." But then why shouldn't a court wait until it is confronted with particularly troubling applications of the Amendment, rather than striking it down across the board?

Finally, Tribe's argument falters a little in its definition of groups. A state may not, he claims, "set some persons apart by declaring that a personal characteristic that they share may not be made the basis for any protection pursuant to the state's laws from any instance of discrimination, however invidious and unwarranted." If Amendment 2 really does sweep this broadly, then he may have a point. But of course, most state laws and policies discriminate against certain groups on the basis of their personal characteristics. In 1979, for example, the Supreme Court upheld as perfectly reasonable the New York City Transit Authority's policy of refusing to hire drug addicts. And couldn't the voters of New York, in their state constitution, prohibit the New York Legislature from overturning the policy by passing an anti-discrimination law for drug addicts? As long as drug addicts retained the right to challenge particular instances of unjustified discrimination under neutral laws, they would hardly be denied "equal protection." Of course, there are plausible arguments that gay men, lesbians and bisexuals should receive more legal protection than drug addicts or left-handed people, because sexual orientation originates in a deeper and morally neutral part of a person's identity, or whatever; but these are difficult and controversial arguments, and Tribe's powerful brief, for strategic reasons, declines to make them.

By reluctantly defending the constitutionality of Amendment 2, at least if it's read narrowly rather than broadly, I don't mean to minimize the indignity of a referendum that singles out a particular group of citizens and denies them the right to seek redress for "claims of discrimination" based on their deepest personal characteristics. Even if the Amendment has merely symbolic rather than practical effects, the symbolism is a stark and public insult to the dignity and equality of homosexual citizens. But the ambiguities of the *Romer* case are the inevitable result of an anxious transitional period, when anti-discrimination protections are often lumped together in the public mind with the travails of affirmative action and when the baseline for equal rights as opposed to special rights is hotly contested. This transitional debate is unlikely to be resolved by judicial fiat, nor should it be. It should be resolved by reasoned cultural and political argument. As the relatively close vote on Amendment 2 suggests, this is by no means a hopeless cause. And as the pro-life movement can attest in the wake of *Roe v. Wade* [the 1973 Supreme Court decision legalizing abortion] there are worse things to be endured than a dramatic defeat by the Supreme Court.

Romer Was Not as Progressive as It Seemed

Joyce Murdoch and Deb Price

*In 2001 lesbian partners and award-winning journalists Joyce
Murdoch and Deb Price published a book examining the impact
of the Supreme Court on gay rights. In looking at the legacy of
the* Romer v. Evans *decision, they noted that the Court seemed
hesitant to apply the ruling to other cases. That ruling struck
down Amendment 2, an amendment to Colorado's state constitution that would have forbidden state and local officials from
enforcing legislation designed specifically to protect gay people
from discrimination. Cincinnati, Ohio, had passed a similar
amendment to its city charter in 1992, and in the wake of the*
Romer *decision, a number of gay people and gay rights organizations challenged the constitutionality of this legislation. Ultimately, these plaintiffs appealed their case to the Supreme Court.
At first, the Court seemed to agree with the plaintiffs, sending
the case back down to the lower court for review in light of the*
Romer *decision. However, as Murdoch and Price reveal in this
viewpoint, when the Sixth Circuit Court reaffirmed its ruling*

Joyce Murdoch and Deb Price, *Courting Justice: Gay Men and Lesbians v. the Supreme
Court*, New York: Basic Books, a member of Perseus Books Group, 2001. Copyright ©
2001 by Joyce Murdoch and Deb Price. Reprinted by permission of Basic Books, a
member of Perseus Books, L.L.C. In the UK and British Commonwealth by permission
of the authors.

upholding the amendment's constitutionality, the Supreme Court seemed to back down, raising questions about the extent of Romer's reach as a precedent.

On June 17, 1996, just four weeks after sternly intoning, "This Colorado cannot do," the same six-justice majority that had struck down Colorado's anti-gay Amendment 2 seemed to add, "And neither can Cincinnati."

The Supreme Court erased a Sixth Circuit decision upholding Cincinnati's very similar anti-gay amendment to its city charter, then sent the case back down "for further consideration in light of *Romer v. Evans*"—code meaning, "Our earlier ruling dictates the outcome of your case."

Those actions seemed to suggest that six justices were committed to using *Romer* on behalf of gay Americans. Perhaps more than anything else, *Romer* gave gay people a promise of fairness. Reading between the lines of *Romer's* soaring prose, it's easy to see Justices [Anthony] Kennedy, [John Paul] Stevens, [Sandra Day] O'Connor, [David] Souter, [Ruth Bader] Ginsburg and [Stephen] Breyer pledging not to let prejudice rule them.

Romer lectured Colorado that there is no gay exception to the Constitution's guarantee of equal protection, that government must not put its stamp of approval on anti-gay animosity. Yet for all its grandeur, that ruling generated more questions than answers: Was the court being honest in signaling gay Americans that it was no longer hostile territory? When push came to shove—as it inevitably would—how many real friends would gay Americans have? Could they count on the *Romer* six—or, at least, five of the six?

For four years, gay Americans waited impatiently to learn whether a majority of the court was really willing to use its first real gay-rights ruling as a cornerstone for decisions moving gay Americans toward full legal equality. When, in June 2000, the Supreme Court finally addressed gay rights again, gay Americans received an unwanted math lesson: On a court where five votes can do anything, gay Americans have four strong allies.

Cincinnati's Anti-gay Amendment

Between *Romer* and that 2000 lesson, the court dealt directly with gay rights only in the Cincinnati case. And in the end, the court chose not to tell Cincinnati what it can or cannot do.

The saga of Cincinnati's anti-gay amendment was almost identical to that of Colorado's Amendment 2 in fencing gay people out of the normal political process by making it more difficult for them than anyone else to seek government help. In 1991, the Cincinnati City Council banned discrimination based on sexual orientation in city employment. The next year the council outlawed such discrimination in private employment, housing and public accommodations.

As a direct result, Take Back Cincinnati—later called Equal Rights Not Special Rights—got an anti-gay amendment to the city's charter onto the ballot. That amendment, known as Issue 3, passed on November 2, 1992, with 62 percent of the vote. Issue 3 declared that city officials "may not enact, adopt, enforce or administer any ordinance, regulation, rule or policy which provides that homosexual, lesbian or bisexual orientation, status, conduct or relationship constitutes, entitles or otherwise provides a person with the basis to have any claim of minority or protected status, quota preference or other preferential treatment."

Equality Foundation of Greater Cincinnati, which had led the fight against Issue 3, joined a housing group, a lesbian mother and four gay men in suing. (One man, Chad Bush, had had a discrimination complaint pending until the city said it could no longer enforce its anti-bias law.)

Federal Judge S. Arthur Spiegel blocked Issue 3 from taking effect, then struck it down as too vague and as a violation of a host of constitutional rights. He denounced "grossly inaccurate" Issue 3 campaign materials that depicted homosexuals as pedophiles and as people whose sexual practices "involve . . . rodents." Building on [Justice William] Brennan's *Rowland* [*v. California Men's Colony*] dissent Spiegel ruled that gay people have "suffered a history of invidious discrimination." Issue 3's purpose, he declared, was to give "effect to private prejudice. This, the Constitution will not tolerate."

As Issue 3 headed to the Sixth Circuit, the anti-gay side recruited Robert Bork and former attorney general Edwin Meese. When the [Bill] Clinton administration refused a gay request to get involved, *The New York Times* accused it of "cowardice." Meanwhile, Cincinnati voters deleted sexual orientation protections from the city's anti-bias law.

The Sixth Circuit's Two Rulings

On May 12, 1995, a Sixth Circuit panel leaned on [*Bowers v.*] *Hardwick* in finding nothing unconstitutional about Issue 3. It ruled the measure might advance "a litany of valid community interests," such as expressing majority "moral views" and enhancing "liberty" for people who want to be free to "dissociate themselves from homosexuals"—that is, free to discriminate.

In August 1995, the Equality Foundation petitioned the Supreme Court, which sat on the request while grappling with *Romer*'s Amendment 2. When the court's June 1996 one-sentence Cincinnati ruling cited *Romer*, that action was "widely regarded as the fatal blow for Issue 3 because the two laws were considered nearly identical," the *Cincinnati Enquirer* noted.

Yet a short dissent by the [Antonin] Scalia-led trio of *Romer* protesters that included [William] Rehnquist and [Clarence] Thomas almost begged the Sixth Circuit to stick to its anti-gay guns. The dissenters pointed to an obvious difference from Amendment 2: Issue 3 was a local, not a state, measure.

(Yet the landmark *Hunter v. Erickson* [1969] ruling had overturned a discriminatory addition to a city charter.)

On October 23, 1997, the same Sixth Circuit panel—Robert Krupansky, Cornelia Kennedy and Alan Norris—shocked observers by again upholding Issue 3. Trying to justify what certainly seemed like a slap at the Supreme Court, the panel claimed *Romer* was not relevant. In contrast to "conscience-shocking" Amendment 2, Issue 3 involved a local measure and "merely prevented homosexuals . . . from obtaining special privileges and preferences" rather than blocking all protection for discrimination, it ruled. Of course, *Romer* had explicitly ruled that Amendment 2 was unconstitutional regardless of whether it canceled all discrimination protections.

Undercutting *Romer*

When Issue 3 bounced back, the Supreme Court ducked, denying *cert[iorari]* [meaning it refused to hear the case] in *Equality Foundation of Greater Cincinnati et al. v. City of Cincinnati* on October 13, 1998. No justice publicly dissented. Yet Stevens, joined by Souter and Ginsburg, issued an extraordinary explanation that, while not citing *Romer*, served to caution against reading the court's inaction as undercutting *Romer*. Denial of *cert*, Stevens stressed, "is not a ruling on the merits. Sometimes such an order reflects nothing more than a conclusion that a particular case may not constitute an appropriate forum in which to decide a significant issue." He added that "confusion" over Issue 3's reach "counsels against" taking the case.

Except for the Sixth Circuit, lower courts had struck down or blocked Amendment 2–style anti-gay initiatives in the wake of *Romer*. The Supreme Court's passivity allowed Cincinnati's Issue 3 to be the only such measure to survive.

Court watcher Arthur Leonard saw Stevens's [unusual] statement as a defensive, strategic move. "It means that those on the court that we like to think of as supportive of gay and lesbian rights didn't have the votes. . . . I've got to believe the problem is with O'Connor and Kennedy," he said, pointing ominously to the most conservative justices in *Romer*'s six-member majority.

CHAPTER 3

Sodomy Laws
Are Unconstitutional

Case Overview

Lawrence v. Texas (2003)

Despite the growth of constitutional law and the sometimes dramatic changes in interpretation of amendments, it is rare for the Supreme Court to explicitly repudiate a previous ruling. The decision in the case of *Lawrence v. Texas* is one of those repudiations.

In September 1998 John Geddes Lawrence and Tyron Garner, residents of a Houston suburb, were discovered having sex by a police officer who entered Lawrence's home on the basis of a report of a man with a gun "going crazy." In fact, the false complaint was filed by a malicious neighbor, but that did not prevent the police officer from arresting the two men under Texas's Homosexual Conduct law. The couple pleaded "no contest" to the charges initially, before a justice of the peace, but they were entitled to ask for a retrial before a criminal court, which they did. At that point they asked that the charges be dismissed as unconstitutional, because the law specifically targeted homosexual but not heterosexual sodomy in violation of the Fourteenth Amendment's equal protection clause and the right to privacy.

Although a three-judge panel of the Texas Court of Appeals agreed with the appellants, the full Court of Appeals overturned that decision, relying in part on the U.S. Supreme Court's *Bowers v. Hardwick* decision, which rejected any inherent right to homosexual conduct. The case then went to the U.S. Supreme Court itself, giving the Court an opportunity to revisit its reasoning in the *Bowers* case.

The case attracted a great deal of attention, and an unusually large number of gay rights and social conservative organizations filed *amici curiae*, or friends of the court briefs urging a decision on one side or the other. In its 6–3 decision, the

Supreme Court agreed with the gay rights groups that the Texas law violated the Fourteenth Amendment rights of the appellants by specifically targeting gay people.

In his majority opinion, Justice Anthony Kennedy specifically overturned *Bowers v. Hardwick*, repudiating its finding that homosexual sodomy is still widely condemned throughout Western civilization. Noting that European attitudes toward homosexuality had changed significantly and that numerous states had repealed their sodomy statutes, Kennedy stated that the *Bowers* decision "was not correct when it was decided, and it is not correct today." He also found that Texas had no legitimate state interest that would justify intruding into this most intimate aspect of its citizens' lives. In her concurrence, Justice Sandra Day O'Connor, who had been in the *Bowers* majority, disagreed somewhat. For her, the issue was equal protection, and she found the Texas law illegitimate purely on the grounds that it did not treat homosexual and heterosexual sodomy the same.

In his dissent, Justice Antonin Scalia disagreed with Kennedy and O'Connor. He declared that the Court's majority had signed on to the "homosexual agenda" and its decision threatened not only any cases decided on the basis of *Bowers*, but virtually the entire legal basis for laws based on sexual morality, from age of consent, to incest, to marriage. In fact, lower courts have been somewhat reluctant to apply the *Lawrence* decision in a number of areas, such as in Alabama's prohibition of sex toys. However, on the specific issue of same-sex marriage, many feel that it did open the door for the Massachusetts Supreme Judicial Court's decision to mandate equal marriage rights for the state's gay citizens in *Goodridge v. Department of Health*, also decided in 2003.

> "Bowers *was not correct when it was decided, and it is not correct today. It ought not to remain binding precedent.*"

The Court's Decision: *Bowers* Was Wrong.

Anthony Kennedy

It is unusual for the Supreme Court to completely reverse an earlier opinion, but in Lawrence v. Texas *the Court quite bluntly reversed* Bowers v. Hardwick. *The central issue in* Lawrence *was the contention that homosexuality was so despised in Western civilization that it could not enjoy the protection that race and religion enjoyed. Justice Anthony Kennedy disagreed. In his majority opinion, he stated that in the nineteenth century, sodomy laws were used to punish rapes and pederasty rather than private, consensual relationships between adults. He also found that the entire European Union had struck down sodomy laws through a decision by the European Court of Human Rights. Finally, he noted that state courts had not used the* Bowers *decision as a precedent in their own decisions. For him, all of this indicated that state governments and the Court had seriously, indeed unconstitutionally, overreached in allowing laws against such intimate, personal conduct as sexual relations between homosexual adults.*

Kennedy has been considered an influential swing vote in both the previous William Rehnquist and the current John Roberts courts. Prior to his appointment as a justice in 1988, he was a practicing attorney and then a professor at the McGeorge School of Law at the University of the Pacific in California.

Anthony Kennedy, majority opinion, *Lawrence v. Texas*, U.S. Supreme Court, June 26, 2003.

Liberty protects the person from unwarranted government intrusions into a dwelling or other private places. In our tradition the State is not omnipresent in the home. And there are other spheres of our lives and existence, outside the home, where the State should not be a dominant presence. Freedom extends beyond spatial bounds. Liberty presumes an autonomy of self that includes freedom of thought, belief, expression, and certain intimate conduct. The instant [current] case involves liberty of the person both in its spatial and more transcendent dimensions. . . .

We conclude the case should be resolved by determining whether the petitioners were free as adults to engage in the private conduct in the exercise of their liberty under the Due Process Clause of the Fourteenth Amendment to the Constitution. For this inquiry we deem it necessary to reconsider the Court's holding in *Bowers* [*v. Hardwick* (1986)].

There are broad statements of the substantive reach of liberty under the Due Process Clause in earlier cases, including *Pierce v. Society of Sisters* (1925), and *Meyer v. Nebraska* (1923); but the most pertinent beginning point is our decision in *Griswold v. Connecticut* (1965).

In *Griswold* the Court invalidated a state law prohibiting the use of drugs or devices of contraception and counseling or aiding and abetting the use of contraceptives. The Court described the protected interest as a right to privacy and placed emphasis on the marriage relation and the protected space of the marital bedroom.

After *Griswold* it was established that the right to make certain decisions regarding sexual conduct extends beyond the marital relationship. In *Eisenstadt v. Baird* (1972), the Court invalidated a law prohibiting the distribution of contraceptives to unmarried persons. The case was decided under the Equal Protection Clause, but with respect to unmarried persons, the Court went on to state the fundamental proposition that the law impaired the exercise of their personal rights. It quoted from the statement of the Court of Appeals finding the law to be in conflict with fundamental human rights, and it followed with this statement of its own:

> It is true that in *Griswold* the right of privacy in question inhered in the marital relationship. . . . If the right of privacy means anything, it is the right of the *individual*, married or single, to be free from unwarranted governmental intrusion into matters so fundamentally affecting a person as the decision whether to bear or beget a child. . . .

Bowers Reconsidered

The Court began its substantive discussion in *Bowers* as follows: "The issue presented is whether the Federal Constitution confers a fundamental right upon homosexuals to engage in sodomy and hence invalidates the laws of the many States that still make such conduct illegal and have done so for a very long time." That statement, we now conclude, discloses the Court's own failure to appreciate the extent of the liberty at stake. To say that the issue in *Bowers* was simply the right to engage in certain sexual conduct demeans the claim the individual put forward, just as it would demean a married couple were it to be said marriage is simply about the right to have sexual intercourse. The laws involved in *Bowers* and here are, to be sure, statutes that purport to do no more than prohibit a particular sexual act. Their penalties and purposes, though, have more far-reaching consequences, touching upon the most private human conduct, sexual behavior, and in the most private of places, the home. The statutes do seek to control a personal relationship that, whether or not entitled to formal recognition in the law, is within the liberty of persons to choose without being punished as criminals.

This, as a general rule, should counsel against attempts by the State, or a court, to define the meaning of the relationship or to set its boundaries absent injury to a person or abuse of an institution the law protects. It suffices for us to acknowledge that adults may choose to enter upon this relationship in the confines of their homes and their own private lives and still retain their dignity as free persons. When sexuality finds overt expression in intimate conduct with another person, the conduct can be but one element in a personal bond that is more enduring. The liberty protected by the Constitution allows homosexual persons the right to make this choice. . . .

Laws prohibiting sodomy do not seem to have been enforced against consenting adults acting in private. A substantial number of sodomy prosecutions and convictions for which there are surviving records were for predatory acts against those who could not or did not consent, as in the case of a minor or the victim of an assault. As to these, one purpose for the prohibitions was to ensure there would be no lack of coverage if a predator committed a sexual assault that did not constitute rape as defined by the criminal law. Thus the model sodomy indictments presented in a 19th-century treatise addressed the predatory acts of an adult man against a minor girl or minor boy. Instead of targeting relations between consenting adults in private, 19th-century sodomy prosecutions typically involved relations between men and minor girls or minor boys, relations between adults involving force, relations between adults implicating disparity in status, or relations between men and animals. . . .

It was not until the 1970's that any State singled out same-sex relations for criminal prosecution, and only nine States have done so. . . . Post-*Bowers* even some of these States did not adhere to the policy of suppressing homosexual conduct. Over the course of the last decades, States with same-sex prohibitions have moved toward abolishing them.

In summary, the historical grounds relied upon in *Bowers* are more complex than the majority opinion and the concurring opinion by Chief Justice [Warren] Burger indicate. Their historical premises are not without doubt and, at the very least, are overstated.

It must be acknowledged, of course, that the Court in *Bowers* was making the broader point that for centuries there have been powerful voices to condemn homosexual conduct as immoral. The condemnation has been shaped by religious beliefs, conceptions of right and acceptable behavior, and respect for the traditional family. For many persons these are not trivial concerns but profound and deep convictions accepted as ethical and moral principles to which they aspire and which thus determine the course of their lives. These considerations do not answer the question before us, however. The issue is whether the majority may use the power of the State to enforce these views on the whole society through operation of the criminal law. "Our obligation is to define the liberty of all, not to mandate our own moral code." . . .

Gay Rights Precedents

The sweeping references by Chief Justice Burger to the history of Western civilization and to Judeo-Christian moral and ethical standards [in his concurring opinion in *Bowers*] did not take account of other authorities pointing in an opposite direction. A committee advising the British Parliament recommended in 1957 repeal of laws punishing homosexual conduct. Parliament enacted the substance of those recommendations 10 years later.

Of even more importance, almost five years before *Bowers* was decided the European Court of Human Rights considered a case with parallels to *Bowers* and to today's case. An adult male resident in Northern Ireland alleged he was a practicing homosexual who desired to engage in consensual homosexual conduct. The laws of Northern Ireland forbade him that right. He alleged that he had been questioned, his home had been searched, and he feared criminal prosecution. The court held that the laws proscribing the conduct were invalid under the European Convention on Human Rights. *Dudgeon v. United Kingdom* (1981). Authoritative in all countries that are members of the Council of Europe (21 nations then, 45 nations now), the decision is at odds with the premise in *Bowers* that the claim put forward was insubstantial in our Western civilization. . . .

The foundations of *Bowers* have sustained serious erosion from our recent decisions in [*Planned Parenthood v.*] *Casey* [1992] and *Romer* [*v. Evans* (1996)]. When our precedent has been thus weakened, criticism from other sources is of greater significance. In the United States criticism of *Bowers* has been substantial and continuing, disapproving of its reasoning in all respects, not just as to its historical assumptions. The courts of five different States have declined to follow it in interpreting provisions in their own state constitutions parallel to the Due Process Clause of the Fourteenth Amendment.

To the extent *Bowers* relied on values we share with a wider civilization, it should be noted that the reasoning and holding in *Bowers* have been rejected elsewhere. The European Court of Human Rights has followed not *Bowers* but its own decision in *Dudgeon v. United Kingdom*. Other nations, too, have taken action consistent with an affirmation of the protected right of homosexual adults to engage in intimate, consensual conduct. The right the petitioners seek in this case has been accepted as an integral part of human freedom in many other countries. There has been no showing that in this country the governmental interest in circumscribing personal choice is somehow more legitimate or urgent. . . .

Flawed Rationale

The rationale of *Bowers* does not withstand careful analysis. In his dissenting opinion in *Bowers* Justice [John Paul] Stevens came to these conclusions:

> Our prior cases make two propositions abundantly clear.
> First, the fact that the governing majority in a State has traditionally viewed a particular practice as immoral is not a sufficient reason for upholding a law prohibiting the prac-

tice; neither history nor tradition could save a law prohibiting miscegenation [mixed-race marriage] from constitutional attack. Second, individual decisions by married persons, concerning the intimacies of their physical relationship, even when not intended to produce offspring, are a form of "liberty" protected by the Due Process Clause of the Fourteenth Amendment. Moreover, this protection extends to intimate choices by unmarried as well as married persons. . . .

Justice Stevens' analysis, in our view, should have been controlling in *Bowers* and should control here.

Bowers was not correct when it was decided, and it is not correct today. It ought not to remain binding precedent. *Bowers v. Hardwick* should be and now is overruled.

The present case does not involve minors. It does not involve persons who might be injured or coerced or who are situated in relationships where consent might not easily be refused. It does not involve public conduct or prostitution. It does not involve whether the government must give formal recognition to any relationship that homosexual persons seek to enter. The case does involve two adults who, with full and mutual consent from each other, engaged in sexual practices common to a homosexual lifestyle. The petitioners are entitled to respect for their private lives. The State cannot demean their existence or control their destiny by making their private sexual conduct a crime. Their right to liberty under the Due Process Clause gives them the full right to engage in their conduct without intervention of the government. "It is a promise of the Constitution that there is a realm of personal liberty which the government may not enter." *Casey*. The Texas statute furthers no legitimate state interest which can justify its intrusion into the personal and private life of the individual.

Had those who drew and ratified the Due Process Clauses of the Fifth Amendment or the Fourteenth Amendment known the components of liberty in its manifold possibilities, they might have been more specific. They did not presume to have this insight. They knew times can blind us to certain truths and later generations can see that laws once thought necessary and proper in fact serve only to oppress. As the Constitution endures, persons in every generation can invoke its principles in their own search for greater freedom.

The judgment of the Court of Appeals for the Texas Fourteenth District is reversed, and the case is remanded for further proceedings not inconsistent with this opinion.

> *So imbued is the Court with the law profession's anti-anti-homosexual culture, that it is seemingly unaware that the attitudes of that culture are not obviously "mainstream."*

Dissenting Opinion: *Bowers* Was Right.

Antonin Scalia

Like the Court majority, Justice Antonin Scalia focused on the Bowers decision in his dissent in Lawrence v. Texas. But for him, the Bowers decision was entirely correct, and he emphatically rejected any need to revise it. He began by focusing on the doctrine of stare decisis (a Latin phrase meaning "to stand by decisions"), by which the Court attempts to uphold previous decisions in order to maintain stability in the jurisprudence. In addition to ignoring such an important legal doctrine, the Court, in Scalia's opinion, was inventing a fundamental right to sodomy without even bothering to explain why. Indeed, the Court was acting not on behalf of the Constitution or the majority of citizens, Scalia argued, but instead purely in conformity with a legal elite that embraced gay rights and gay people far more than either the Founding Fathers or the American populace.

After serving in the Richard Nixon and Gerald Ford administrations, Antonin Scalia taught law at the University of Chicago, Georgetown University, and Stanford University, developing a reputation as a vigorous proponent of judicial restraint and interpreting the Constitution according to the founders'

Antonin Scalia, dissenting opinion, *Lawrence v. Texas*, U.S. Supreme Court, 539 U.S. 558, June 26, 2003.

original intent. He was appointed to the Supreme Court in 1986 by President Ronald Reagan.

I begin with the Court's surprising readiness to reconsider a decision rendered a mere 17 years ago in *Bowers v. Hardwick*. I do not myself believe in rigid adherence to *stare decisis* in constitutional cases; but I do believe that we should be consistent rather than manipulative in invoking the doctrine. Today's opinions in support of reversal do not bother to distinguish—or indeed, even bother to mention—the paean to *stare decisis* coauthored by three Members of today's majority in *Planned Parenthood v. Casey*. There, when *stare decisis* meant preservation of judicially invented abortion rights, the widespread criticism of *Roe* [*v. Wade*] was strong reason to *reaffirm* it. . . .

Today's approach to *stare decisis* invites us to overrule an erroneously decided precedent (including an "intensely divisive" decision) *if*: (1) its foundations have been "eroded" by subsequent decisions; (2) it has been subject to "substantial and continuing" criticism; and (3) it has not induced "individual or societal reliance" that counsels against overturning. The problem is that *Roe* itself—which today's majority surely has no disposition to overrule—satisfies these conditions to at least the same degree as *Bowers*. . . .

Misapplying the Due Process Clause

Having decided that it need not adhere to *stare decisis*, the Court still must establish that *Bowers* was wrongly decided and that the Texas statute, as applied to petitioners, is unconstitutional.

Texas Penal Code Ann. §21.06(a) (2003) undoubtedly imposes constraints on liberty. So do laws prohibiting prostitution, recreational use of heroin, and, for that matter, working more than 60 hours per week in a bakery. But there is no right to "liberty" under the Due Process Clause, though today's opinion repeatedly makes that claim. . . .

Our opinions applying the doctrine known as "substantive due process" hold that the Due Process Clause prohibits States from infringing *fundamental* liberty interests, unless the infringement is narrowly tailored to serve a compelling state interest. . . .

Bowers held, first, that criminal prohibitions of homosexual sodomy are not subject to heightened scrutiny because they do not implicate a "fundamental right" under the Due Process Clause. . . .

The Court today does not overrule this holding. Not once does it describe homosexual sodomy as a "fundamental right" or a "fundamental liberty interest," nor does it subject the Texas statute to strict scrutiny. Instead, having failed to establish that the right to homosexual sodomy is "'deeply rooted in this Nation's history and tradition,'" the Court concludes that the application of Texas's statute to petitioners' conduct fails the rational-basis test, and overrules *Bowers'* holding to the contrary. "The Texas statute furthers no legitimate state interest which can justify its intrusion into the personal and private life of the individual." . . .

History Justifies the *Bowers* Decision

The Court's description of "the state of the law" at the time of *Bowers* only confirms that *Bowers* was right. The Court points to *Griswold v. Connecticut*, (1965). But that case *expressly disclaimed* any reliance on the doctrine of "substantive due process," and grounded the so-called "right to privacy" in penumbras of constitutional provisions *other than* the Due Process Clause. *Eisenstadt v. Baird*, (1972), likewise had nothing to do with "substantive due process"; it invalidated a Massachusetts law prohibiting the distribution of contraceptives to unmarried persons solely on the basis of the Equal Protection Clause. Of course *Eisenstadt* contains a well-known dictum relating to the "right to privacy," but this referred to the right, recognized in *Griswold*—a right penumbral to the *specific* guarantees in the Bill of Rights, and not a "substantive due process" right. . . .

After discussing the history of antisodomy laws, the Court proclaims that, "it should be noted that there is no longstanding history in this country of laws directed at homosexual conduct as a distinct matter." This observation in no way casts into doubt the "definitive [historical] conclusion," on which *Bowers* relied: that our Nation has a longstanding history of laws prohibiting *sodomy in general*—regardless of whether it was performed by same-sex or opposite-sex couples:

"It is obvious to us that neither of these formulations would extend a fundamental right to homosexuals to engage in acts of consensual sodomy. Proscriptions against that conduct have ancient roots. *Sodomy* was a criminal offense at common law and was forbidden by the laws of the original 13 States when they ratified the Bill of Rights. In 1868, when the Fourteenth Amendment was ratified, all but 5 of the 37 States in the Union had *criminal sodomy laws*. In fact, until 1961, all 50 States outlawed *sodomy*, and today, 24 States and the District of Columbia continue to provide criminal penalties for *sodomy* performed in private and between consenting adults. Against this background, to claim that a right to engage in such conduct is 'deeply rooted in this Nation's history and tradition' or 'implicit in the concept of ordered liberty' is, at best, facetious."

It is (as *Bowers* recognized) entirely irrelevant whether the laws in our long national tradition criminalizing homosexual sodomy were "directed at homosexual conduct as a distinct matter." Whether homosexual sodomy was prohibited by a law targeted at same-sex sexual relations or by a more general law prohibiting both homosexual and heterosexual sodomy, the only relevant point is that it *was* criminalized—which suffices to establish that homosexual sodomy is not a right "deeply rooted in our Nation's history and tradition." The Court today agrees that homosexual sodomy was criminalized and thus does not dispute the facts on which *Bowers actually* relied.

Next the Court makes the claim, again unsupported by any citations, that "[l]aws prohibiting sodomy do not seem to have been enforced against consenting adults acting in private." The key qualifier here is "acting in private"—since the Court admits that sodomy laws *were* enforced against consenting adults (although the Court contends that prosecutions were "infrequent,"). I do not know what "acting in private" means; surely consensual sodomy, like heterosexual intercourse, is rarely performed on stage. If all the Court means by "acting in private" is "on private premises, with the doors closed and windows covered," it is entirely unsurprising that evidence of enforcement would be hard to come by. (Imagine the circumstances that would enable a search warrant to be obtained for a residence on the ground that there was probable cause to believe that consensual sodomy was then and there occurring.) Surely that lack of evidence would not sustain the proposition that consensual sodomy on private premises with the doors closed and windows covered was regarded as a "fundamental right," even though all other consensual sodomy was criminalized. There are 203 prosecutions for consensual, adult homosexual sodomy reported in the West Reporting system and official state reporters from the years 1880–1995. There are also records of 20 sodomy prosecutions and 4 executions during the colonial period. *Bowers'* conclusion that homosexual sodomy is not a fundamental right "deeply rooted in this Nation's history and tradition" is utterly unassailable. . . .

An Attack on All Morals Legislation

I turn now to the ground on which the Court squarely rests its holding: the contention that there is no rational basis for the law here under attack. This proposition is so out of accord with our jurisprudence—indeed, with the jurisprudence of *any* society we know—that it requires little discussion.

The Texas statute undeniably seeks to further the belief of its citizens that certain forms of sexual behavior are "immoral and unacceptable,"—the same interest furthered by criminal laws against fornication, bigamy, adultery, adult incest, bestiality, and obscenity. *Bowers* held that this *was* a legitimate state interest. The Court today reaches the opposite conclusion. The Texas statute, it says, "furthers *no legitimate state interest* which can justify its intrusion into the personal and private life of the individual," (emphasis addded). The Court embraces instead Justice [John Paul] Stevens' declaration in his *Bowers* dissent, that "the fact that the governing majority in a State has traditionally viewed a particular practice as immoral is not a sufficient reason for upholding a law prohibiting the practice." This effectively decrees the end of all morals legislation. If, as the Court asserts, the promotion of majoritarian sexual morality is not even a *legitimate* state interest, none of the above-mentioned laws can survive rational-basis review. . . .

Taking Sides in the Culture War

Today's opinion is the product of a Court, which is the product of a law-profession culture, that has largely signed on to the so-called homosexual agenda, by which I mean the agenda promoted by some homosexual activists directed at eliminating the moral opprobrium that has traditionally attached to homosexual conduct. I noted in an earlier opinion the fact that the American Association of Law Schools (to which any reputable law school *must* seek to belong) excludes from membership any school that refuses to ban from its job-interview facilities a law firm (no matter how small) that does not wish to hire as a prospective partner a person who openly engages in homosexual conduct.

One of the most revealing statements in today's opinion is the Court's grim warning that the criminalization of homosexual conduct is "an invitation to subject homosexual persons to discrimination both in the public and in the private spheres." It is clear from this that the Court has taken sides in the culture war, departing from its role of assuring, as neutral observer, that the democratic rules of engagement are observed. Many Americans do not want persons who openly engage in homosexual conduct as partners in their business, as scoutmasters for their children, as teachers in their children's schools, or as boarders in their home. They view this as protecting themselves and their families from a lifestyle that they believe to be immoral and destructive. The Court views it as "discrimination" which it is the function of our judgments to deter. So imbued is the Court with the law profession's anti-anti-homosexual culture, that it is seemingly unaware that the attitudes of that culture are not obviously "mainstream"; that in most States what the Court calls "discrimination" against those who engage in homosexual acts is perfectly legal; that proposals to ban such "discrimination" under Title VII have repeatedly been rejected by Congress, and that in some cases such "discrimination" is a constitutional right, see *Boy Scouts of America v. Dale* (2000).

Let me be clear that I have nothing against homosexuals, or any other group, promoting their agenda through normal democratic means. Social perceptions of sexual and other morality change over time, and every group has the right to persuade its fellow citizens that its view of such matters is the best. That homosexuals have achieved some success in that enterprise is attested to by the fact that Texas is one of the few remaining States that criminalize private, consensual homosexual acts. But persuading one's fellow citizens is one thing and imposing one's views in absence of democratic majority will is something else. I would no more *require* a State to criminalize homosexual acts—or, for that matter, display *any* moral disapprobation of them—than I would *forbid* it to do so. What Texas has chosen to do is well within the range of traditional democratic action, and its hand should not be stayed through the invention of a brand-new "constitutional right" by a Court that is impatient of democratic change. It is indeed true that "later generations can see that laws once thought necessary and proper in fact serve only to oppress," and when that happens, later generations can repeal those laws. But it is the premise of our system that those judgments are to be made by the people, and not imposed by a governing caste that knows best.

One of the benefits of leaving regulation of this matter to the people rather than to the courts is that the people, unlike judges, need not carry things to their logical conclusion. The people may feel that their disapprobation of homosexual conduct is strong enough to disallow homosexual marriage, but not strong enough to criminalize private homosexual acts— and may legislate accordingly. The Court today pretends that it possesses a similar freedom of action, so that we need not fear judicial imposition of homosexual marriage, as has recently occurred in Canada (in a decision that the Canadian Government has chosen not to appeal). At the end of its opinion—after having laid waste the foundations of our rational-basis jurisprudence—the Court says that the present case "does not involve whether the government must give formal recognition to any relationship that homosexual persons seek to enter." Do not believe it. More illuminating than this bald, unreasoned disclaimer is the progression of thought displayed by an earlier passage in the Court's opinion, which notes the constitutional protections afforded to "personal decisions relating to *marriage*, procreation, contraception, family relationships, child rearing, and education," and then declares that "[p]ersons in a homosexual relationship may seek autonomy for these purposes, just as heterosexual persons do." Today's opinion dismantles the structure of constitutional law that has permitted a distinction to be made between heterosexual and homosexual unions, insofar as formal recognition in marriage is concerned. If moral disapprobation of homosexual conduct is "no legitimate state interest" for purposes of proscribing that conduct; and if, as the Court coos (casting aside all pretense of neutrality), "[w]hen sexuality finds overt expression in intimate conduct with another person, the conduct can be but one element in a personal bond that is more enduring," what justification could there possibly be for denying the benefits of marriage to homosexual couples exercising "[t]he liberty protected by the Constitution?" Surely not the encouragement of procreation, since the sterile and the elderly are allowed to marry. This case "does not involve" the issue of homosexual marriage only if one entertains the belief that principle and logic have nothing to do with the decisions of this Court. Many will hope that, as the Court comfortingly assures us, this is so.

The matters appropriate for this Court's resolution are only three: Texas's prohibition of sodomy neither infringes a "fundamental right" (which the Court does not dispute), nor is unsupported by a rational relation to what the Constitution considers a legitimate state interest, nor denies the equal protection of the laws. I dissent.

> *"Radical social change does not arrive or gain acceptance overnight. But once the tipping point is past, it comes, ineluctably."*

The Court Is Challenging Traditional Morality, and Rightly So

Edward Lazarus

Looking back at both the 1986 Bowers v. Hardwick *decision that upheld sodomy laws, and the 2003* Lawrence v. Texas *decision that struck them down, legal commentator Edward Lazarus notes a dramatic change in societal attitudes. He states that the* Bowers *outcome was essentially decided by Justice Lewis Powell's swing vote, and was based in part on Powell's admitted ignorance stemming from his belief that he did not even know any gay people (despite the fact that one of his law clerks was gay). Lazarus contrasts this with Anthony Kennedy, another generally conservative justice, who in the majority opinion in* Lawrence *labels laws banning homosexual expression as bigoted and oppressive. While there is still homophobic bigotry in society, and on the Supreme Court itself, Lazarus asserts, the* Lawrence *decision both reflects and furthers a new era in which blatant bigotry against gay people is much less acceptable, both socially and constitutionally.*

Edward Lazarus, "The Changing Battlefield in the Gay Marriage War," *Findlaw.com*, March 4, 2004, http://writ.news.findlaw.com/lazarus/20040304.html. Reproduced by permission.

A onetime clerk for Justice Harry Blackmun, Lazarus is the author of Closed Chambers, *an insider's look at the Supreme Court. He is a frequent legal commentator on various television and radio programs.*

As the cultural war heats up over the issue of gay marriage, it is worth reflecting on how much and how quickly the battlefield has changed.

Only 20 years ago, gay bashing was commonplace in "polite" society, and the idea of gay rights had yet to make a dent in the nation's political consciousness. Now, however, one of the most conservative Presidents in U.S. history [i.e., George W. Bush]—despite proposing a constitutional amendment outlawing gay marriage—tiptoes around the morality of homosexuality, and feels compelled to accept the possibility of gay and lesbian civil unions.

In every civil rights movement, there comes a time when public figures and the cultural elite no longer countenance blatant acts of discrimination: when it is no longer okay to use the "N-word," or wolf-whistle at a woman, or display a cigar store Indian. These are tipping points (to borrow a fashionable phrase) in the push to equality—the point when the rock of Sisyphus stops falling back, and instead rolls over the summit and sweeps downhill towards the promised land of full and equal rights.

I cannot say whether the gay rights movement has yet reached that summit. But, if not, it is surely close. And to understand how far the gay rights movement has come, one need look no farther that the U.S. Supreme Court, the institution of the national government most responsible for the change.

Looking Back at *Bowers*

In 1986, the Supreme Court took up the famous—indeed, notorious—case of *Bowers v. Hardwick.* The case arose when Michael Hardwick was arrested for violating Georgia's criminal ban on sodomy after police entered his home and found him in bed with another man.

In defending himself against the criminal charge, Hardwick challenged the constitutionality of Georgia's ban on sodomy. Specifically, he argued that his constitutional right to privacy included a right to engage in homosexual sex and, thus, meant that Georgia's sodomy law should be struck down.

As a legal matter, Hardwick's case involved one of the most difficult areas of constitutional law. The Constitution does not explicitly recognize a "right to privacy." Nonetheless, a line of Supreme Court precedents—including the ever-controversial *Roe v. Wade* [legalizing abortion]—have found what amounts, more or less, to just such a right.

These cases have held that the Constitution's due process clause—which states that no person shall be deprived of "liberty" without due process of law—includes a right to make certain deeply personal decisions without interference from the government. The issue in Hardwick's case was whether that zone of constitutional liberty was broad enough to include a right to engage in consensual homosexual sex within the confines of a private home.

Inside the Court, Hardwick's case provoked polar opposite reactions. The four more liberal justices (William Brennan, Thurgood Marshall, Harry Blackmun, and John Paul Stevens) were comfortable embracing Hardwick's privacy claim.

These justices saw Hardwick's argument as a natural extension of the Court's privacy jurisprudence—which protected both decisions related to sex (such as the choice to use contraception or obtain an abortion), and also placed great emphasis on the privacy of the home (which is especially sacrosanct from searches under Fourth Amendment jurisprudence). By their lights, those two strands of decisions converged when—as in Hardwick's case—both sex and privacy were at issue, and made for a clear result: Hardwick's act could not constitutionally be criminalized.

Warren Burger's Role

On the other side, however, Chief Justice Warren Burger was apoplectic at the thought that the Court might read into the Constitution a right to engage in homosexual sex. Three other justices (Byron White, William Rehnquist, and Sandra Day O'Connor) had strong philosophical aversions to expanding the right to privacy—and so they, too, lined up against Hardwick.

With these justices split 4–4, the swing vote in Hardwick belonged to Lewis Powell, the Court's consistent centrist. He genuinely didn't know what to do. Powell believed generally in a constitutional right to privacy. But extending it to homosexual sex made him uncomfortable.

As Powell freely confessed to his colleagues, he was operating in ignorance. Powell did not think he had ever actually *met* a homosexual—even though one of his own clerks that year was gay.

Powell's indecision provoked an urgent response from Chief Justice Burger. He sent Powell a private letter pleading with him to vote against *Hardwick*. In the letter, [Burger] argued in no uncertain terms that extending the right to privacy to homosexual sex would threaten the very foundation of western civilization. And, in the end, Burger's lobbying carried the day.

Powell voted with Burger, and the Supreme Court denied Hardwick's claim by a 5–4 vote. Justice Byron White's brief and dismissive majority opinion reflects at best a callous indifference (and perhaps a latent hostility) to the concerns of homosexuals caught between sexual desire and criminal sanction.

But it is Burger's concurrence that deserves special note. There, Burger wrote approvingly that [eighteenth-century English legal scholar William] "Blackstone described 'the infamous crime against nature' as an offense of 'deeper malignity' than rape, a heinous act 'the very mention of which is a disgrace to human nature,' and 'a crime not fit to be named.'"

In addition, Burger opined that "To hold that the act of homosexual sodomy is somehow protected as a fundamental right would be to cast aside millennia of moral teaching."

Same Issue, Different Decision

Fast forward to 2003—when the very issue decided in *Hardwick* returns to the Supreme Court, in the case of *Lawrence v. Texas.*

John Geddes Lawrence, like Hardwick before him, was surprised in his bedroom by local police while engaging in homosexual sex. Charged with violating Texas's criminal statute outlawing gay sex, Lawrence raises the same due process defense Hardwick had raised unsuccessfully 17 years earlier (as well as a claim based on the Fourteenth Amendment's Equal Protection clause).

Yet Lawrence wins at the Supreme Court—and not by a 5–4 vote. He wins by a vote of 6–3. Moreover, the Court specifically overrules its previous decision in *Hardwick.*

Not only that, the majority opinion—written by the social and political conservative Justice Anthony Kennedy—disavows Burger's *Hardwick* concurrence, and resoundingly affirms the choice to be gay as a central part of the Constitution's promise of liberty.

The homophobic voice of Burger can still be heard, but this time, it is only the voice of two Justices—Justice [Antonin] Scalia and Chief Justice Rehnquist. Justice Antonin Scalia's outraged dissent defends the right of states to express moral disapproval of homosexuality. It complains that "[t]oday's opinion is the product of a Court, which is the product of a law-profession culture, that has largely signed on to the so-called homosexual agenda, by which I mean the agenda promoted by some homosexual activists directed at eliminating the moral opprobrium that has traditionally attached to homosexual conduct."

Even Scalia feels compelled to add a "Not that there's anything wrong with that" disclaimer—writing "Let me be clear that I have nothing against homosexuals, or any other group, promoting their agenda through normal democratic means." But it's simply not convincing, given the tone of the rest of his opinion.

It is Justice Clarence Thomas's dissent that is more telling. Though Thomas joins Scalia's dissent, he also distances himself from Scalia through his own, separate dissent. And there, Thomas goes out of his way to describe Texas's law banning gay sex as "uncommonly silly."

Indeed, Thomas goes so far as to imagine himself a legislator taking a pro-gay-rights stance! He writes, "If I were a member of the Texas Legislature, I would vote to repeal [this law]. Punishing someone for expressing his sexual preference through noncommercial consensual conduct with another adult does not appear to be a worthy way to expend valuable law enforcement resources."

In sum, then, we have the gay plaintiff winning 6–3; a conservative justice turning in a passionate opinion vindicating gay rights; another conservative Justice, Justice O'Connor, concurring with that pro-gay rights opinion; a defensive dissenting conservative Justice borrowing from [comedian Jerry] Seinfeld; and another dissenting Justice openly taking a libertarian stance when it comes to gay sex.

We have indeed come a long way, baby.

A Moral Revolution

Lawrence reflects a moral as well as legal revolution. Between 1986 and 2003, the Court moved from outright hostility towards gay rights to a warm embrace.

And nothing captures this shift better than the change at the center of the Court. In 1986, Powell, the swing vote on a relatively liberal Court, was totally clueless about—and, at best, indifferent to—homosexuality. In 2003, Kennedy, a justice near the center of a much more conservative Court, bluntly denounces laws banning the sexual expression of homosexuality as a form of bigotry and "oppression."

Such moral pronouncements from the Supreme Court do matter. They move the marker of what is socially acceptable, and such movements develop a momentum of their own.

After the Supreme Court issued its 1954 decision in *Brown v. Board of Education* [abolishing racial segregation in public facilities], it took 13 years before the Court took the additional step, in *Loving v. Virginia,* of declaring unconstitutional laws banning interracial marriage.

Radical social change does not arrive or gain acceptance overnight. But once the tipping point is past, it comes, ineluctably. And, so, almost surely, it will again.

> What sexual liberationists, "gay" or "straight," wish to abolish is the legal concept of marriage as a "one-flesh union."

The Court Cannot Create a Right to Consensual Sex

Robert P. George

Writing shortly before the Lawrence v. Texas *decision was handed down, legal scholar and Princeton professor Robert P. George finds deep flaws in the plaintiffs' contention that the Court should strike down sodomy laws. According to George, the issue comes down to marital versus nonmarital relations. By asking the Supreme Court to grant a constitutional right to a kind of sexual relationship outside of marriage, George fears that the plaintiffs are opening a dangerous new interpretation of the Constitution, one that could provide constitutional protection to all extramarital relations, including adultery, polygamy, and prostitution. Indeed, he writes, that* Lawrence *is part of an ideological campaign against marriage itself, one that could seriously erode the institution and endanger future generations of children. While states are not obligated to penalize extramarital sex, George argues, they have every right to do so, and by denying them that right the Court would defy all long-held traditions and could irreparably damage one of the most important institutions holding American society together: heterosexual marriage.*

In *Lawrence v. Texas*, proponents of judicial activism in the cause of liberal ideological goals are asking the Supreme Court of the United States to do something the justices have never done before: Throw the mantle of constitutional protection around a type of non-marital sex act.

The Supreme Court has never recognized a right to fornication, adultery, or any other form of sexual misconduct. True, it has included within a generalized right of privacy a right of married and even non-married people to purchase and use contraceptives; but the justices have made plain that their rulings in the contraception cases do not protect illicit sex acts. In *Griswold v. Connecticut* (1965), the Court ruled that prohibiting contraceptives to married couples interferes in a damaging way in the marital relationship and is therefore not a constitutionally permissible way of combating adultery or other forms of sexual vice. In *Eisenstadt v. Baird* (1972), the justices held that pregnancy, or the risk of pregnancy, may not be used as a means of punishing or deterring fornication. Nothing in either case forbids states from banning outright adultery, fornication, or other immoral sex acts. On the contrary, as constitutional scholar Gerard Bradley has noted, *Eisenstadt* and other cases expressly acknowledge the authority of government to prohibit such acts.

In *Bowers v. Hardwick* (1986), the Court explicitly declined to create a right to homosexual sodomy. (The justices did not address the question of heterosexual sodomy, inside or outside of marriage, since it was not necessary to do so to resolve the case.) If, as the petitioners in *Lawrence* demand, the Court now reverses *Bowers* and manufactures a constitutional right to sodomy (as a specification of the right of privacy or on some other basis), it will be a truly radical departure—granting constitutional protection to a type of non-marital sex act (indeed, in this case, an intrinsically non-marital act).

In the event that it takes such a step, the Court will face a question: If *some* types of non-marital sex acts are protected by the Constitution, *and others are not,* what is the principle or criterion (allegedly derived from the Constitution itself) by which judges are to decide which types merit protection and which do not?

Marriage Relationship Protected

Under prevailing law, the marriage relationship enjoys constitutional protection; sex outside the marital bond does not. This does not mean that states are obligated to criminalize all or any extramarital sex acts. What it means, simply, is that it is up to the states to decide whether to ban any such acts, and, if so, which ones. In making the determination to forbid or tolerate this or that form of sexual misconduct, be it fornication, adultery (with or without spousal consent), sodomy, prostitution, consensual adult incest, etc., legislators are free to bring to bear their best prudential judgment in weighing the pros and cons of alternative policy options. As with the regulation of gambling and drugs, the federal courts claim no jurisdiction to interfere in the policymaking process.

But if the Supreme Court dismantles prevailing law, with what criterion or set of criteria will it replace *marriage* as the principle by which courts distinguish constitutionally protected from unprotected sexual conduct? Some plausible alternative principle must be identified to justify the judiciary's authority to displace legislative judgments.

Consent: An Insufficient Answer

The leading alternative is the notion of *consent*. Fundamental social libertarians hold that acts of *any* type, including *any* type of sex act, should be legally permissible so long as the parties involved consent to participating in them and others are not directly harmed. Those who believe that the founding fathers wrote the ideology of fundamental social libertarianism into the Constitution (albeit with invisible ink) maintain that the constitutional right of privacy immunizes all consensual sex acts from state prohibitions.

If this is true, then not only sodomy, but also fornication, adultery (e.g., spouse swapping, "swinging"), polygamy, group sex, prostitution, adult brother-sister or parent-child incest, and (depending on one's views about the rights of animals and their capacity to consent) bestiality are protected as specifications of the constitutional right of privacy. All of these acts and practices are, or can be, consensual. If consent provides the standard of inclusion within the right of privacy, they must all be admitted.

Pennsylvania Senator Rick Santorum caused a firestorm [in 2003] simply by pointing this out (as had Justice Byron White, the John F. Kennedy appointee who wrote the Court's opinion in the *Bowers* case). Democratic partisans and opponents of traditional norms of sexual morality jumped on him with accusations of "intolerance" and "bigotry." A few Republican "moderates" piled on. But where is the flaw in the premises or logic of Santorum's (and Justice White's) argument? Can his critics identify a principle by reference to which sodomy falls within the ambit of constitutional protection and other non-marital sex acts fall outside it?

Clearly the idea of consent cannot provide such a principle. Nor can the concept of *tradition*, for no type of non-marital sexual conduct is sanctioned by "the history and conscience of the American people." On the contrary, our tradition is precisely to treat *marriage* as the principle of rectitude in sexual matters, and to single out the marital bond for unique legal protection.

So, if neither *marriage*, nor *consent*, nor *tradition* provides the criterion for deciding which forms of consensual sexual conduct are to enjoy constitutional protection and which are not, then *what does provide the criterion?* If Sen. Santorum is wrong to suggest that *there is no such criterion*, his critics should be able easily to refute his argument by producing it. Why haven't they done so?

They haven't done so, and won't be able to do so, because Rick Santorum is right: There is no principle that courts can employ in picking and choosing among the range of possible consensual non-marital forms of sexual conduct for purposes of assigning constitutional protection. If marriage is overthrown as the principle that distinguishes protected from unprotected conduct in matters of sexuality, it will have to be replaced, in the end, by the idea of consent. No non-arbitrary grounds will be available for deciding that sodomy and fornication are "in," but consensual adultery, group sex, commercial sex, etc., are "out." The rational pressure for consistency will move courts in the direction of imposing by judicial fiat the agenda of fundamental social libertarianism. And that was Rick Santorum's point.

Destroying Marriage Is the Goal

Advocates of sexual liberation will say, of course, that retaining marriage as the criterion of constitutional protection is unfair since persons of the same sex cannot legally marry each other. But this objection reveals their ultimate goal: the destruction of marriage as it has been understood in Western law and culture and the substitution of a new concept in line with sexual-liberationist ideology.

This ideology is deeply hostile to the idea of marriage as uniting one man and one woman in a permanent bond of the type that is *per se* suitable for the generation, nurturance, and upbringing of children. Yet it is the fact that marriage is naturally ordered to the generation, nurturance, and upbringing of children that largely justifies the law's concern with marriage at all. No society can afford to be indifferent about the terms and conditions under which children are brought into being, cared for, and guided into adulthood.

What sexual liberationists, "gay" or "straight," wish to abolish is the legal concept of marriage as a "one-flesh union" made possible by the sexual complementarity of a husband

and wife whose physical union is the biological basis of the comprehensive sharing of life that marriage is meant to be. This concept of marriage has deep intellectual roots in both Jerusalem and Athens—in Biblical principles and the great Western tradition of philosophical reflection. Today, however, it is considered outdated by people who view sex as essentially a matter of satisfaction seeking and marriage as a mere legal convention that can be revised and redefined to accommodate the range of subjective sexual "preferences" people happen to have.

Anyone who recognizes the critical significance of strong marriages and families to the well being of children and the social health of the nation should shudder at the prospect of a radical redefinition of the already much-battered institution of marriage. Although we are only a little more than 30 years into the sexual revolution that began in earnest in the 1960s, the legacy of sexual-liberationist ideology is measurable in ruined relationships and broken lives. We need policies that uphold and strengthen marriage, not those that further erode it in our law and culture. On this, too, Rick Santorum is right.

CHAPTER 4

The Question of Same-Sex Marriage

Case Overview

Goodridge v. Department of
Public Health (2003)

Should gay people be subject to prison sentences because of their sex lives? Should states have the power to prevent anti-discrimination ordinances if they apply to gay people? Are the Boy Scouts allowed to dismiss gay members? Is the army? These are deeply emotional and often personal questions with profound legal, religious, and political implications. They have all provoked enormous controversy, and judicial decisions in this area have often sparked outrage on one side or the other. But few court cases, in any area, have provoked the kind of political backlash launched by *Goodridge v. Department of Public Health*.

At the center of the case was the issue of same-sex marriage, a startling and new idea for many people. This was more than gays asking for an end to discrimination or striking down a hurdle (such as Colorado's Amendment 2) designed specifically to restrict gay rights. Many people had already moved toward a belief that sodomy laws were archaic, and many were at least theoretically in favor of equal rights for gay people. Others were disapproving but took a live-and-let-live attitude. Then came the first gay marriage cases.

The first major case occurred in the early 1970s, when the Minnesota Supreme Court denied a marriage license to two male plaintiffs. The plaintiffs appealed, but the U.S. Supreme Court denied that any federal right was at issue in *Baker v. Nelson*, in effect affirming the Minnesota court's decision. In a few other states in the mid-1970s, some licenses were issued to same-sex couples, but legislatures immediately moved to define marriage as being strictly between a man and a woman. The issue seemed to die down until 1993 when the Hawaii

State Supreme Court ruled that the state's equal protection clause meant that marriage licenses must be issued to same-sex couples who seek them.

Throughout the country, opponents of gay marriage denounced the decision as "judicial activism" and declared that virtually any gay couple could go to Hawaii and get married, forcing other states to accept the marriage. Congress rushed to pass the Defense of Marriage Act, signed by President Bill Clinton, which defined marriage as strictly heterosexual under federal law, and prevented the federal government from recognizing same-sex marriages granted by the states. For many, these fears were exaggerated and based on a false reading of the Constitution's "full faith and credit clause," but the political fallout was very real. As it turned out, the people of Hawaii passed an anti-same-sex marriage amendment, so the question remained moot, but already things were changing in other states.

In 1999, the Vermont Supreme Court ruled that gay couples must receive all the legal and civil protections of straight marriage partners. The legislature voted down an attempt to pass gay marriage, but voted to create civil unions to meet the Court's ruling in 2000. And in May 2004, the Supreme Judicial Court of Massachusetts ruled that the state must recognize same-sex marriage. A subsequent decision in 2006 ruled that the same-sex marriages of out-of-state residents would be void in their home states, unless those states specifically recognized such marriages. Despite attempts to overturn the decision through a constitutional amendment, same-sex marriage seems fairly secure in the state, with majorities supporting it in recent polls and a number of legislators backing away from their previous opposition.

On the other side, by mid-2006 nineteen states had passed constitutional amendments explicitly barring same-sex marriage. For many, the issue remains highly charged, and there is speculation that the Republican Party in particular has used the issue as a way to get out the vote and win elections. A number of analysts believe that the issue hurt 2004 Democratic presidential candidate John Kerry, who personally opposes same-sex marriage but supports civil unions. Republicans continue to promote same-sex marriage bans in states, however, a Federal Marriage Amendment that would have outlawed gay marriage everywhere, failed to gain majority votes in both the House and Senate in June 2006.

At the same time, according to experts, a majority of Americans now support the idea of some legal recognition for gay couples, a dramatic change from even a few years ago. The entire issue of civil unions for gay couples and gay families, however, remains unsettled, volatile, and the source undoubtedly of future controversy in the courts and the wider political realm.

> "Without the right to marry—or more
> properly, the right to choose to marry—
> one is excluded from the full range of
> human experience and denied full pro-
> tection of the laws."

The Court's Decision: Massachusetts Cannot Restrict Marriage to Heterosexual Couples.

Margaret H. Marshall

*Same-sex couples sought marriage in Hawaii and gained civil
unions in Vermont, but the Supreme Judicial Court of Massachusetts was the first to find a right in its state constitution for
same-sex couples to marry. Although the court rejected the ini-
tial claim that the legislature did not mean to exclude same-sex
couples from marriage, the majority found that the Commonwealth of Massachusetts constitution's guarantees of equal protection mandated marriage rights for gay and lesbian people.
Chief Justice Margaret H. Marshall explained in her opinion
that by denying same-sex couples the many rights that married
couples enjoyed, the state was denying them the equal protection
of its laws. She also rejected the state's contention that this denial was necessary for the encouragement of procreation, the
protection of children, or the limiting of scarce state resources.*

 *Born in South Africa, Marshall came to the United States in
1968 to pursue graduate studies at Harvard University and a
law degree at Yale. She practiced law, becoming a partner at*

Margaret H. Marshall, majority opinion, *Goodridge v. Department of Public Health*, Supreme Court of Massachusetts, 2003.

Choate, Hall and Stewart, and later served as general counsel for Harvard. She joined the Massachusetts Supreme Judicial Court in 1996 and was appointed the court's first female chief justice in 1999.

Marriage is a vital social institution. The exclusive commitment of two individuals to each other nurtures love and mutual support; it brings stability to our society. For those who choose to marry, and for their children, marriage provides an abundance of legal, financial, and social benefits. In return it imposes weighty legal, financial, and social obligations. The question before us is whether, consistent with the Massachusetts Constitution, the Commonwealth may deny the protections, benefits, and obligations conferred by civil marriage to two individuals of the same sex who wish to marry. We conclude that it may not. The Massachusetts Constitution affirms the dignity and equality of all individuals. It forbids the creation of second-class citizens. In reaching our conclusion we have given full deference to the arguments made by the Commonwealth. But it has failed to identify any constitutionally adequate reason for denying civil marriage to same-sex couples.

We are mindful that our decision marks a change in the history of our marriage law. Many people hold deep-seated religious, moral, and ethical convictions that marriage should be limited to the union of one man and one woman, and that homosexual conduct is immoral. Many hold equally strong religious, moral, and ethical convictions that same-sex couples are entitled to be married, and that homosexual persons should be treated no differently than their heterosexual neighbors. Neither view answers the question before us. Our concern is with the Massachusetts Constitution as a charter of governance for every person properly within its reach. "Our Obligation is to define the liberty of all, not to mandate our own moral code." *Lawrence v. Texas* (2003).

Whether the Commonwealth may use its formidable regulatory authority to bar same-sex couples from civil marriage is a question not previously addressed by a Massachusetts appellate court. It is a question the United States Supreme Court left open as a matter of Federal law in *Lawrence*, where it was not an issue. There, the Court affirmed that the core concept of common human dignity protected by the Fourteenth Amendment to the United States Constitution precludes government intrusion into the deeply personal realms of consensual adult expressions of intimacy and one's choice of an intimate partner. The Court also reaffirmed the central role that decisions whether to marry or have children bear in shaping one's identity. The Massachusetts Constitution is, if anything, more protective of individual liberty and equality than the Federal Constitution; it may demand broader protection for fundamental rights; and it is less tolerant of government intrusion into the protected spheres of private life.

Barred access to the protections, benefits, and obligations of civil marriage, a person who enters into an intimate, exclusive union with another of the same sex is arbitrarily deprived of membership in one of our community's most rewarding and cherished institutions. That exclusion is incompatible with the constitutional principles of respect for individual autonomy and equality under law. . . .

Marriage Licensing Statute

Although the plaintiffs refer in passing to "the marriage statutes," they focus, quite properly, on G.L. [General Laws] c. 207, the marriage licensing statute, which controls entry into civil marriage. As a preliminary matter, we summarize the provisions of that law.

General Laws c. 207 is both a gatekeeping and a public records statute. It sets minimum qualifications for obtaining a marriage license and directs city and town clerks, the registrar, and the department to keep and maintain certain "vital records" of civil marriages. The gatekeeping provisions of G.L. c. 207 are minimal. They forbid marriage of individuals within certain degrees of consanguinity, and polygamous marriages. They prohibit marriage if one of the parties has communicable syphilis, and restrict the circumstances in which a person under eighteen years of age may marry. . . .

The record-keeping provisions of G.L. c. 207 are more extensive. Marriage applicants file standard information forms and a medical certificate in any Massachusetts city or town clerk's office and tender a filing fee. The clerk issues the marriage license, and when the marriage is solemnized, the individual authorized to solemnize, the marriage adds additional information to the form and returns it (or a copy) to the clerk's office . . . (this completed form is commonly known as the "marriage certificate"). The clerk sends a copy of the information to the registrar, and that information becomes a public record.

In short, for all the joy and solemnity that normally attend a marriage, G.L. c. 207, governing entrance to marriage, is a licensing law. The plaintiffs argue that because nothing in that licensing law specifically prohibits marriages between persons of the same sex, we may interpret the statute to permit "qualified same sex couples" to obtain marriage licenses, thereby avoiding the question whether the law is constitutional. This claim lacks merit. . . .

Far from being ambiguous, the undefined word "marriage," as used in G.L. c. 207 confirms the General Court's intent to hew to the term's common-law and quotation meaning concerning the genders of the marriage partners. . . .

The Primary Issue

The larger question is whether, as the department claims, government action that bars same-sex couples from civil marriage constitutes a legitimate exercise of the State's authority to regulate conduct, or whether, as the plaintiffs claim, this categorical marriage exclusion violates the Massachusetts Constitution. We have recognized the long-standing statutory understanding, derived from the common law, that "marriage" means the lawful union of a woman and a man. But that history cannot and does not foreclose the constitutional question.

The plaintiffs' claim that the marriage restriction violates the Massachusetts Constitution can be analyzed in two ways. Does it offend the Constitution's guarantees of equality before the law? Or do the liberty and due process provisions of the Massachusetts Constitution secure the plaintiffs' right to marry their chosen partner? In matters implicating marriage, family life, and the upbringing of children, the two constitutional concepts frequently overlap, as they do here. . . .

We begin by considering the nature of civil marriage itself. Simply put, the government creates civil marriage. In Massachusetts, civil marriage is, and since pre-Colonial days has been, precisely what its name implies: a wholly secular institution. . . . No religious ceremony has ever been required to validate a Massachusetts marriage.

In a real sense, there are three partners to every civil marriage: two willing spouses and an approving State. . . .

Without question, civil marriage enhances the "welfare of the community." It is a "social institution of the highest importance." *French v. McAnarney* [1935]. Civil marriage anchors an ordered society by encouraging stable relationships over transient ones. It is central to the way the Commonwealth identifies individuals, provides for the orderly distribution of property, ensures that children and adults are cared for and supported whenever possible from private rather than public funds, and tracks important epidemiological and demographic data.

Marriage also bestows enormous private and social advantages on those who choose to marry. Civil marriage is at once a deeply personal commitment to another human being and a highly public celebration of the ideals of mutuality, companionship, intimacy, fidelity, and family. "It is an association that promotes a way of life, not causes; a harmony in living, not political faiths; a bilateral loyalty, not commercial or social projects." *Griswold v. Connecticut* (1965). Because it fulfils yearnings for security, safe haven, and connection that express our common humanity, civil marriage is an esteemed institution, and the decision whether and whom to marry is among life's momentous acts of self-definition.

Tangible as well as intangible benefits flow from marriage. The marriage license grants valuable property rights to those who meet the entry requirements, and who agree to what might otherwise be a burdensome degree of government regulation of their activities. . . .

The benefits accessible only by way of a marriage license are enormous, touching nearly every aspect of life and death. The department states that "hundreds of statutes" are related to marriage and to marital benefits. . . .

Marriage as a Civil Right

It is undoubtedly for these concrete reasons, as well for its intimately personal significance, that civil marriage has long been termed a "civil right." . . . The United States Supreme Court has described the right to marry as "of fundamental importance for all individuals" and as "part of the fundamental 'right of privacy' implicit in the Fourteenth Amendment's Due Process Clause." *Zablocki v. Redhail* (1978).

Without the right to marry—or more properly, the right to choose to marry—one is excluded from the full range of human experience and denied full protection of the laws for one's "avowed commitment to an intimate and lasting human relationship." *Baker v. State* [1999]. . . .

The department argues that no fundamental right or "suspect" class is at issue here, and rational basis is the appropriate standard of review. For the reasons we explain below, we conclude that the marriage ban does not meet the rational basis test for either due process or equal protection. Because the statute does not survive rational basis review, we do not consider the plaintiffs' arguments that this case merits strict judicial scrutiny.

The department posits three legislative rationales for prohibiting same-sex couples from marrying: (1) providing a "favorable setting for procreation"; (2) ensuring the optimal setting for child rearing, which the department defines as "a two-parent family with one parent of each sex"; and (3) preserving scarce State and private financial resources. We consider each in turn.

Procreation Rationale

The judge in the Superior Court endorsed the first rationale, holding that "the state's interest in regulating marriage is based on the traditional concept that marriage's primary purpose is procreation." This is incorrect. Our laws of civil marriage do not privilege procreative heterosexual intercourse between married people above every other form of adult intimacy and every other means of creating a family. General Laws c. 207 contains no requirement that the applicants for a marriage license attest to their ability or intention to conceive children by coitus. Fertility is not a condition of marriage, nor is it grounds for divorce. People who have never consummated their marriage, and never plan to, may be and stay married. . . . While it is certainly true that many, perhaps most, married couples have children together (assisted or unassisted), it is the exclusive and permanent commitment of the marriage partners to one another, not the begetting of children, that is the sine qua non of civil marriage.

Moreover, the Commonwealth affirmatively facilitates bringing children into a family regardless of whether the intended parent is married or unmarried, whether the child is adopted or born into a family, whether assistive technology was used to conceive the child, and whether the parent or her partner is heterosexual, homosexual, or bisexual. If procreation were a necessary component of civil marriage, our statutes would draw a tighter circle around the permissible bounds of nonmarital child bearing and the creation of families by noncoital means. The attempt to isolate procreation as "the source of a fundamental right to marry," overlooks the integrated way in which courts have examined the complex and overlapping realms of personal autonomy, marriage, family life, and child rearing. Our jurisprudence recognizes that, in these nuanced and fundamentally private areas of life, such a narrow focus is inappropriate.

The "marriage is procreation" argument singles out the one unbridgeable difference between same-sex and opposite-sex couples, and transforms that difference into the essence of legal marriage. Like "Amendment 2" to the Constitution of Colorado, which effectively denied homosexual persons equality under the law and full access to the political process, the marriage restriction impermissibly "identifies persons by a single trait and then denies them protection across the board." *Romer v. Evans* (1996). In so doing, the State's action confers an official stamp of approval on the destructive stereotype that same-sex relationships are inherently unstable and inferior to opposite-sex relationships and are not worthy of respect.

Children's Welfare Rationale

The department's first stated rationale, equating marriage with unassisted heterosexual procreation, shades imperceptibly into its second: that confining marriage to opposite-sex couples ensures that children are raised in the "optimal" setting. Protecting the welfare of children is a paramount State policy. Restricting marriage to opposite-sex couples, however, cannot plausibly further this policy. "The demographic changes of the past century make it difficult to speak of an average American family. The composition of families varies greatly from household to household." *Troxel v. Granville* (2000). Massachusetts has responded supportively to "the changing realities of the American family," and has moved vigorously to strengthen the modern family in its many variations. . . .

The department has offered no evidence that forbidding marriage to people of the same sex will increase the number of couples choosing to enter into opposite-sex marriages in order to have and raise children. There is thus no rational relationship between the marriage statute and the Commonwealth's proffered goal of protecting the "optimal" child rearing unit. Moreover, the department readily concedes that people in same-sex couples may be "excellent" parents. These couples (including four of the plaintiff couples) have children for the reasons others do—to love them, to care for them, to nurture them. But the task of child rearing for same-sex couples is made infinitely harder by their status as outliers to the marriage laws. While establishing the parentage of children as soon as possible is crucial to the safety and welfare of children, same-sex couples must undergo the sometimes lengthy and intrusive process of second-parent adoption to establish their joint parentage. While the enhanced income provided by marital benefits is an important source of security and stability for married couples and their children, those benefits are denied to families headed by same-sex couples. While the laws of divorce provide clear and reasonably predictable guidelines for child support, child custody, and property division on dissolution of a marriage, same-sex couples who dissolve their relationships find themselves and their children in the highly unpredictable terrain of equity jurisdiction. Given the wide range of public benefits reserved only for married couples, we do not credit the department's contention that the absence of access to civil marriage amounts to little more than an inconvenience to same-sex couples and their children. Excluding same-sex couples from civil marriage will not make children of opposite-sex marriages more secure, but it does prevent children of same-sex couples from enjoying the immeasurable advantages that flow from the assurance of "a stable family structure in which children will be reared, educated, and socialized."

No one disputes that the plaintiff couples are families, that many are parents, and that the children they are raising, like all children, need and should have the fullest opportunity to grow up in a secure, protected family unit. Similarly, no one disputes that, under the rubric of marriage, the State provides a cornucopia of substantial benefits to married parents and their children. The preferential treatment of civil marriage reflects the Legislature's conclusion that marriage "is the foremost setting for the education and socialization of children" precisely because it "encourages parents to remain committed to each other and to their children as they grow."

In this case, we are confronted with an entire, sizeable class of parents raising children who have absolutely no access to civil marriage and its protections because they are forbidden from procuring a marriage license. It cannot be rational under our laws, and indeed it is not permitted, to penalize children by depriving them of State benefits because the State disapproves of their parents' sexual orientation.

Financial Rationale

The third rationale advanced by the department is that limiting marriage to opposite-sex couples furthers the Legislature's interest in conserving scarce State and private financial resources. The marriage restriction is rational, it argues, because the General Court logically could assume that same-sex couples are more financially independent than married couples and thus less needy of public marital benefits, such as tax advantages, or private marital benefits, such as employer-financed health plans that include spouses in their coverage.

An absolute statutory ban on same-sex marriage bears no rational relationship to the goal of economy. First, the departments's conclusory generalization—that same-sex couples are less financially dependent on each other than opposite-sex couples—ignores that many same-sex couples, such as many of the plaintiffs in this case, have children and other dependents (here, aged parents) in their care. The department does not contend, nor could it, that these dependents are less needy or deserving than the dependents of married couples. Second, Massachusetts marriage laws do not condition receipt of public and private financial benefits to married individuals on a demonstration of financial dependence on each other; the benefits are available to married couples regardless of whether they mingle their finances or actually depend on each other for support.

The department suggests additional rationales for prohibiting same-sex couples from marrying, which are developed by some amici [friends of the court; i.e., legal advisers]. It argues that broadening civil marriage to include same-sex couples will trivialize or destroy the institution of marriage as it has historically been fashioned. Certainly our decision today marks a significant change in the definition of marriage as it has been inherited from the common law, and understood by many societies for centuries. But it does not disturb the fundamental value of marriage in our society.

Here, the plaintiffs seek only to be married, not to undermine the institution of civil marriage. They do not want marriage abolished. They do not attack the binary nature of marriage, the consanguinity provisions, or any of the other gatekeeping provisions of the marriage licensing law. Recognizing the right of an individual to marry a person of the same sex will not diminish the validity or dignity of opposite-sex marriage, any more than recognizing the right of an individual to marry a person of a different race devalues the marriage of a person who marries someone of her own race. If anything, extending civil marriage to same-sex couples reinforces the importance of marriage to individuals and communities. That same-sex couples are willing to embrace marriage's solemn obligations of exclusivity, mutual support, and commitment to one another is a testament to the enduring place of marriage in our laws and in the human spirit. . . .

Harm of the Marriage Ban

The marriage ban works a deep and scarring hardship on a very real segment of the community for no rational reason. The absence of any reasonable relationship between, on the one hand, an absolute disqualification of same-sex couples who wish to enter into civil marriage and, on the other, protection of public health, safety, or general welfare, suggests that the marriage restriction is rooted in persistent prejudices against persons who are (or who are believed to be) homosexual. "The Constitution cannot control such prejudices but neither can it tolerate them. Private biases may be outside the reach of the law, but the law cannot, directly or indirectly, give them effect." *Palmore v. Sidoti* (1984). Limiting the protections, benefits, and obligations of civil marriage to opposite-sex couples violates the basic premises of individual liberty and equality under law protected by the Massachusetts Constitution. . . .

We construe civil marriage to mean the voluntary union of two persons as spouses, to the exclusion of all others. This reformulation redresses the plaintiffs' constitutional injury and furthers the aim of marriage to promote stable, exclusive relationships. It advances the two legitimate State interests the department has identified: providing a stable setting for child rearing and conserving State resources. It leaves intact the Legislature's broad discretion to regulate marriage.

In their complaint the plaintiffs request only a declaration that their exclusion and the exclusion of other qualified same-sex couples from access to civil marriage violates Massachusetts law. We declare that barring an individual from the protections, benefits, and obligations of civil marriage solely because that person would marry a person of the same sex violates the Massachusetts Constitution. We vacate the summary judgment for the department. We remand this case to the Superior Court for entry of judgment consistent with this opinion. Entry of judgment shall be stayed for 180 days to permit the Legislature to take such action as it may deem appropriate in light of this opinion.

> *"While the institution of marriage is deeply rooted in the history and traditions of our country and our State, the right to marry someone of the same sex is not."*

Dissenting Opinion: The Courts Have No Right to Redefine Marriage.

Robert J. Cordy

In his dissent to Goodridge v. Department of Public Health, *Massachusetts Supreme Judicial Court justice Robert J. Cordy questions all the assumptions of the majority opinion, from the fundamental right to marry to the right of privacy to the idea that gay parents are inherently disadvantaged by the Massachusetts marriage statutes. Given these challenges, Cordy finds that the state's Supreme Judicial Court has no right to overrule the wisdom of the legislature in restricting marriage to opposite-sex couples. For him, this is the fundamental issue: whether the legislature's restrictions are so clearly unreasonable that the court must step in. He argues that they are in fact quite reasonable, and that the court's attempt to substitute its own judgment is simply judicial activism that is unjustified and dangerous.*

In addition to private legal practice, Robert J. Cordy has held a number of government posts, including federal prosecutor, associate general counsel for the State Ethics Commission, and chief of the U.S. Attorney's Public Corruption Unit. He was appointed to the Supreme Judicial Court in 2001.

Robert J. Cordy, dissenting opinion, *Goodridge v. Department of Public Health*, Supreme Court of Massachusetts, 2003.

The court's opinion concludes that the Department of Public Health has failed to identify any "constitutionally adequate reason" for limiting civil marriage to opposite-sex unions, and that there is no "reasonable relationship" between a disqualification of same-sex couples who wish to enter into a civil marriage and the protection of public health, safety, or general welfare. Consequently, it holds that the marriage statute cannot withstand scrutiny under the Massachusetts Constitution. Because I find these conclusions to be unsupportable in light of the nature of the rights and regulations at issue, the presumption of constitutional validity and significant deference afforded to legislative enactments, and the "undesirability of the judiciary substituting its notions of correct policy for that of a popularly elected . . . Legislature" responsible for making such policy, *Zayre Corp. v. Attorney Gen.* (1977), I respectfully dissent. Although it may be desirable for many reasons to extend to same-sex couples the benefits and burdens of civil marriage (and the plaintiffs have made a powerfully reasoned case for that extension), that decision must be made by the Legislature, not the court.

If a statute either impairs the exercise of a fundamental right protected by the due process or liberty provisions of our State Constitution, or discriminates based on a constitutionally suspect classification such as sex, it will be subject to strict scrutiny when its validity is challenged. If it does neither, a statute "will be upheld if it is 'rationally related to a legitimate State purpose.'" This test, referred to in State and Federal constitutional jurisprudence as the "rational basis test," is virtually identical in substance and effect to the test applied to a law promulgated under the State's broad police powers (pursuant to which the marriage statutes and most other licensing and regulatory laws are enacted): that is, the law is valid if it is reasonably related to the protection of public health, safety, or general welfare.

The Massachusetts marriage statute does not impair the exercise of a recognized fundamental right, or discriminate on the basis of sex in violation of the equal rights amendment to the Massachusetts Constitution. Consequently, it is subject to review only to determine whether it satisfies the rational basis test. Because a conceivable rational basis exists upon which the Legislature could conclude that the marriage statute furthers the legitimate State purpose of ensuring, promoting, and supporting an optimal social structure for the bearing and raising of children, it is a valid exercise of the State's police power. . . .

Civil marriage is an institution created by the State. In Massachusetts, the marriage statutes are derived from English common law, and were first enacted in colonial times. They were enacted to secure public interests and not for religious purposes or to promote personal interests or aspirations. As the court notes in its opinion, the institution of marriage is "the legal union of a man and woman as husband and wife," and it has always been so under Massachusetts law, colonial or otherwise.

Redefining a Fundamental Right

The plaintiffs contend that because the right to choose to marry is a "fundamental" right, the right to marry the person of one's choice, including a member of the same sex, must also be a "fundamental" right. While the court stops short of deciding that the right to marry someone of the same sex is "fundamental" such that strict scrutiny must be applied to any statute that impairs it, it nevertheless agrees with the plaintiffs that the right to choose to marry is of fundamental importance ("among the most basic" of every person's "liberty and due process rights") and would be "hollow" if an individual was foreclosed from "freely choosing the person with whom to share . . . the . . . institution of civil marriage." Hence, it concludes that a marriage license cannot be denied to an individual who wishes to marry someone of the same sex. In reaching this result the court has transmuted the "right" to marry into a right to change the institution of marriage itself. This feat of reasoning succeeds only if one accepts the proposition that the definition of the institution of marriage as a union between a man and a woman is merely "conclusory", rather than the basis on which the "right" to partake in it has been deemed to be of fundamental importance. In other words, only by assuming that "marriage" includes the union of two persons of the same sex does the court conclude that restricting marriage to opposite-sex couples infringes on the "right" of same-sex couples to "marry."

The plaintiffs ground their contention that they have a fundamental right to marry a person of the same sex in a long line of Supreme Court decisions, that discuss the importance of marriage. In context, all of these decisions and their discussions are about the "fundamental" nature of the institution of marriage as it has existed and been understood in this country, not as the court has redefined it today. Even in that context, its "fundamental" nature is derivative of the nature of the interests that underlie or are associated with it. An examination of those interests reveals that they are either not shared by same-sex couples or not implicated by the marriage statutes.

Supreme Court cases that have described marriage or the right to marry as "fundamental" have focused primarily on the underlying interest of every individual in procreation, which, historically, could only legally occur within the construct of marriage because sexual intercourse outside of marriage was a criminal act. In *Skinner v. Oklahoma* [1942], the first case to characterize marriage as a "fundamental" right, the Supreme Court stated, as its rationale for striking down a sterilization statute, that "[m]arriage and procreation are fundamental to the very existence of the race." In concluding that a sterilized individual "is forever deprived of a basic liberty," the Court was obviously referring to procreation rather than marriage.... Similarly, in *Loving v. Virginia* [1967], in which the United States Supreme Court struck down Virginia's anti-miscegenation statute, the court implicitly linked marriage with procreation in describing marriage as "fundamental to our very existence." ...

Because same-sex couples are unable to procreate on their own, any right to marriage they may possess cannot be based on their interest in procreation, which has been essential to the Supreme Court's denomination of the right to marry as fundamental....

Misinterpreting Privacy Rights

The marriage statute, which regulates only the act of obtaining a marriage license, does not implicate privacy in the sense that it has found constitutional protection under Massachusetts and Federal law. It does not intrude on any right that the plaintiffs have to privacy in their choices regarding procreation, an intimate partner or sexual relations. The plaintiffs' right to privacy in such matters does not require that the State officially endorse their choices in order for the right to be constitutionally vindicated.

Although some of the privacy cases also speak in terms of personal autonomy, no court has ever recognized such an open-ended right. "That many of the rights and liberties protected by the Due Process Clause sound in personal autonomy does not warrant the sweeping conclusion that any and all important, intimate, and personal decisions are so protected...." *Washington v. Glucksberg* (1997). Such decisions are protected not because they are important, intimate, and personal, but because the right or liberty at stake is "so deeply rooted in our history and traditions, or so fundamental to our concept of constitutionally ordered liberty" that it is protected by due process. Accordingly, the Supreme Court has concluded that while the decision to refuse unwanted medical treatment is fundamental, *Cruzan v. Director, Mo. Dep't of Health* (1990) because it is deeply rooted in our nation's history and tradition, the equally personal and profound decision to commit suicide is not because of the absence of such roots. *Washington v. Glucksberg.*

While the institution of marriage is deeply rooted in the history and traditions of our country and our State, the right to marry someone of the same sex is not. No matter how personal or intimate a decision to marry someone of the same sex might be, the right to make it is not guaranteed by the right of personal autonomy.

The protected right to freedom of association, in the sense of freedom of choice "to enter into and maintain certain intimate human relationships," *Roberts v. United States Jaycees,* (1984) (as an element of liberty or due process rather than free speech), is similarly limited and unimpaired by the marriage statute. As recognized by the Supreme Court, that right affords protection only to "certain kinds of highly personal relationships," such as those between husband and wife, parent and child, and among close relatives, that "have played a critical role in the culture and traditions of the Nation," and are "deeply rooted in this Nation's history and tradition." *Moore v. East Cleveland* (1977). Unlike opposite-sex marriages, which have deep historic roots, or the parent-child relationship, which reflects a "strong tradition" founded on "the history and culture of Western civilization" and "is now established beyond debate as an enduring American tradition," *Wisconsin v. Yodar* (1972); or extended family relationships, which have been "honored throughout our history," *Moore v. East Cleveland,* same-sex relationships, although becoming more accepted, are certainly not so "deeply rooted in this Nation's history and tradition" as to warrant such enhanced constitutional protection. . . .

Statute Does Not Interfere with Child Rearing

Finally, the constitutionally protected interest in child rearing, recognized in *Meyer v. Nebraska*, (1923); *Pierce v. Society of Sisters*, (1925); and *Care & Protection of Robert* [1990], is not implicated or infringed by the marriage statute here. The fact that the plaintiffs cannot marry has no bearing on their independently protected constitutional rights as parents which, as with opposite-sex parents, are limited only by their continued fitness and the best interests of their children. *Bezio v. Patenaude*, (1980) (courts may not use parent's sexual orientation as reason to deny child custody).

Because the rights and interests discussed above do not afford the plaintiffs any fundamental right that would be impaired by a statute limiting marriage to members of the opposite sex, they have no fundamental right to be declared "married" by the State.

Insofar as the right to marry someone of the same sex is neither found in the unique historical context of our Constitution nor compelled by the meaning ascribed by this court to the liberty and due process protections contained within it, should the court nevertheless recognize it as a fundamental right? The consequences of deeming a right to be "fundamental" are profound, and this court, as well as the Supreme Court, has been very cautious in recognizing them. Such caution is required by separation of powers principles. If a right is found to be "fundamental," it is, to a great extent, removed from "the arena of public debate and legislative action"; utmost care must be taken when breaking new ground in this field "lest the liberty protected by the Due Process Clause be subtly transformed into the policy preferences of [judges]." *Washington v. Glucksberg*. . . .

Link Between Marriage and Procreation

The institution of marriage provides the important legal and normative link between heterosexual intercourse and procreation on the one hand and family responsibilities on the other. The partners in a marriage are expected to engage in exclusive sexual relations, with children the probable result and paternity presumed. . . . Whereas the relationship between mother and child is demonstratively and predictably created and recognizable through the biological process of pregnancy and childbirth, there is no corresponding process for creating a relationship between father and child. Similarly, aside from an act of heterosexual intercourse nine months prior to childbirth, there is no process for creating a relationship between a man and a woman as the parents of a particular child. The institution of marriage fills this void by formally binding the husband-father to his wife and child, and imposing on him the responsibilities of fatherhood. . . . The alternative, a society without the institution of marriage, in which heterosexual intercourse, procreation, and child care are largely disconnected processes, would be chaotic.

The marital family is also the foremost setting for the education and socialization of children. Children learn about the world and their place in it primarily from those who raise them, and those children eventually grow up to exert some influence, great or small, positive or negative, on society. The institution of marriage encourages parents to remain committed to each other and to their children as they grow, thereby encouraging a stable venue for the education and socialization of children. . . .

Legislature's Reasonableness

We must assume that the legislature (1) might conclude that the institution of civil marriage has successfully and continually provided this structure over several centuries; (2) might consider and credit studies that document negative consequences that too often follow children either born outside of marriage or raised in households lacking either a father or a mother figure, and scholarly commentary contending that children and families develop best when mothers and fathers are partners in their parenting; and (3) would be familiar with many recent studies that variously: support the proposition that children raised in intact families headed by same-sex couples fare as well on many measures as children raised in similar families headed by opposite-sex couples, support the proposition that children of same-sex couples fare worse on some measures; or reveal notable differences between the two groups of children that warrant further study.

We must also assume that the Legislature would be aware of the critiques of the methodologies used in virtually all of the comparative studies of children raised in these different environments, cautioning that the sampling populations are not representative, that the observation periods are too limited in time, that the empirical data are unreliable, and that the hypotheses are too infused with political or agenda driven bias. . . .

Taking all of this available information into account, the Legislature could rationally conclude that a family environment with married opposite-sex parents remains the optimal social structure in which to bear children, and that the raising of children by same-sex couples, who by definition cannot be the two sole biological parents of a child and cannot provide children with a parental authority figure of each gender, presents an alternative structure for child rearing that has not yet proved itself beyond reasonable scientific dispute to be as optimal as the biologically based marriage norm. . . .

The Legislature could conclude that redefining the institution of marriage to permit same-sex couples to marry would impair the State's interest in promoting and supporting heterosexual marriage as the social institution that it has determined best normalizes, stabilizes, and links the acts of procreation and child rearing. While the plaintiffs argue that they only want to take part in the same stabilizing institution, the Legislature conceivably could conclude that permitting their participation would have the unintended effect of undermining to some degree marriage's ability to serve its social purpose. . . .

As long as marriage is limited to opposite-sex couples who can at least theoretically procreate, society is able to communicate a consistent message to its citizens that marriage is a (normatively) necessary part of their procreative endeavor; that if they are to procreate, then society has endorsed the institution of marriage as the environment for it and for the subsequent rearing of their children; and that benefits are available explicitly to create a supportive and conducive atmosphere for those purposes. If society proceeds similarly to recognize marriages between same-sex couples who cannot procreate, it could be perceived as an abandonment of this claim, and might result in the mistaken view that civil marriage has little to do with procreation: just as the potential of procreation would not be necessary for a marriage to be valid, marriage would not be necessary for optimal procreation and child rearing to occur. In essence, the Legislature could conclude that the consequence of such a policy shift would be a diminution in society's ability to steer the acts of procreation and child rearing into their most optimal setting. . . .

The court recognizes this concern, but brushes it aside with the assumption that permitting same-sex couples to marry "will not diminish the validity or dignity of opposite-sex marriage," and that "we have no doubt that marriage will continue to be a vibrant and revered institution." Whether the court is correct in its assumption is irrelevant. What is relevant is that such predicting is not the business of the courts. A rational Legislature, given the evidence, could conceivably come to a different conclusion, or could at least harbor rational concerns about possible unintended consequences of a dramatic redefinition of marriage. . . .

While "the Massachusetts Constitution protects matters of personal liberty against government intrusion at least as zealously, and often more so than does the Federal Constitution," this case is not about government intrusions into matters of personal liberty. It is not about the rights of same-sex couples to choose to live together, or to be intimate with each other, or to adopt and raise children together. It is about whether the State must endorse and support their choices by changing the institution of civil marriage to make its benefits, obligations, and responsibilities applicable to them. While the courageous efforts of many have resulted in increased dignity, rights, and respect for gay and lesbian members of our community, the issue presented here is a profound one, deeply rooted in social policy, that must, for now, be the subject of legislative not judicial action.

> "When people talk about "gay mar-
> riage," they miss the point. This isn't
> about gay marriage. It's about mar-
> riage. It's about family. It's about love."

The Case for Marriage

Andrew Sullivan

*In a deeply personal statement, one of the chief proponents of
same-sex marriage, Andrew Sullivan, reveals his own reason for
insisting on marriage rights rather than civil unions or domestic
partnerships for gay people. Written shortly after the* Goodridge
*decision, Sullivan's article does not address the case itself so
much as the thinking, and emotion, behind the various lawsuits
challenging the exclusion of gay marriages in various states. Formerly editor of the* New Republic, *Sullivan maintains a Web log
in which he continues to argue passionately for same-sex marriage, as well as discussing numerous other political and social
issues.*

What's in a name?

Perhaps the best answer is a memory.

As a child, I had no idea what homosexuality was. I grew
up in a traditional home—Catholic, conservative, middle class.
Life was relatively simple: education, work, family. I was
brought up to aim high in life, even though my parents hadn't
gone to college. But one thing was instilled in me. What matters is not how far you go in life, how much money you make,
how big a name you make for yourself. What really matters is

Andrew Sullivan, "The M-Word, Time," *Time*, February 10, 2004, pp. 322–324. Copyright © 2004 Time, Inc. All rights reserved. Reproduced by permission.

family, and the love you have for one another. The most important day of your life was not graduation from college or your first day at work or a raise or even your first house. The most important day of your life was when you got married. It was on that day that all your friends and all your family got together to celebrate the most important thing in life: your happiness, your ability to make a new home, to form a new but connected family, to find love that puts everything else into perspective.

But as I grew older, I found that this was somehow not available to me. I didn't feel the things for girls that my peers did. All the emotions and social rituals and bonding of teenage heterosexual life eluded me. I didn't know why. No one explained it. My emotional bonds to other boys were one-sided; each time I felt myself falling in love, they sensed it, pushed it away. I didn't and couldn't blame them. I got along fine with my buds in a non-emotional context; but something was awry, something not right. I came to know almost instinctively that I would never be a part of my family the way my siblings one day might be. The love I had inside me was unmentionable, anathema—even, in the words of the Church I attended every Sunday, evil. I remember writing in my teenage journal one day: "I'm a professional human being. But what do I do in my private life?"

Retreating into Solitude

So, like many gay men of my generation, I retreated. I never discussed my real life. I couldn't date girls and so immersed myself in schoolwork, in the debate team, school plays, anything to give me an excuse not to confront reality. When I looked toward the years ahead, I couldn't see a future. There was just a void. Was I going to be alone my whole life? Would I ever have a "most important day" in my life? It seemed impossible, a negation, an undoing. To be a full part of my family I had to somehow not be me. So like many gay teens, I withdrew, became neurotic, depressed, at times close to suicidal. I shut myself in my room with my books, night after night, while my peers developed the skills needed to form real relationships, and loves. In wounded pride, I even voiced a rejection of family and marriage. It was the only way I could explain my isolation.

It took years for me to realize that I was gay, years later to tell others, and more time yet to form any kind of stable emotional bond with another man. Because my sexuality had emerged in solitude—and without any link to the idea of an actual relationship—it was hard later to reconnect sex to love and self-esteem. It still is. But I persevered, each relationship slowly growing longer than the last, learning in my twenties and thirties what my straight friends found out in their teens. But even then, my parents and friends never asked the question they would have asked automatically if I were straight: so when are you going to get married? When is your relationship going to be public? When will we be able to celebrate it and affirm it and support it? In fact, no one—no one—has yet asked me that question.

It's About Marriage

When people talk about "gay marriage," they miss the point. This isn't about gay marriage. It's about marriage. It's about family. It's about love. It isn't about religion. It's about civil marriage licenses—available to atheists as well as believers. These family values are not options for a happy and stable life. They are necessities. Putting gay relationships in some other category—civil unions, domestic partnerships, civil partnerships, whatever—may alleviate real human needs, but, by their very euphemism, by their very separateness, they actually build a wall between gay people and their own families. They put back the barrier many of us have spent a lifetime trying to erase.

It's too late for me to undo my own past. But I want above everything else to remember a young kid out there who may even be reading this now. I want to let him know that he doesn't have to choose between himself and his family any more. I want him to know that his love has dignity, that he does indeed have a future as a full and equal part of the human race. Only marriage will do that. Only marriage can bring him home.

Same-Sex Marriage Advocates Will Continue to Push for a Wider Application of *Goodridge*

Stanley Kurtz

A longtime opponent of same-sex marriage and contributing editor to the National Review, *Stanley Kurtz argues that one large problem with decisions like* Goodridge *is that they will be wrongly exploited. Noting that many out-of-state residents applied for licenses to marry in Massachusetts, Kurtz fears that the decision has opened up the door to gay marriage in many more states. Even more worrisome, he finds, is same-sex marriage advocates supporting illegal provocations, such as the mayor of San Francisco's decision to marry gay couples on his own authority. For Kurtz, aggressive activists and dishonest commentators undermine any assurances that* Goodridge *will be restricted to Massachusetts residents. The only way to prevent the spread of gay marriage from state to state is with a Federal Marriage Amendment.*

Defiance of the law is rapidly becoming the leitmotif of the gay-marriage movement.

It's not that gay-marriage supporters are generally less law-abiding than others. The root of the problem is that propo-

Stanley Kurtz, "Marriage Mayhem," *National Review Online*, May 20, 2004. Reproduced by permission.

nents of gay marriage see their cause as parallel to the civil-rights movement of the early 1960s. That analogy is badly flawed. But if you buy it, then it's perfectly alright to disobey the law in order to nationalize gay marriage.

This is why it's foolish to put faith in laws that supposedly prevent gay marriage in Massachusetts from spilling over into other states. When it comes to same-sex marriage, it barely matters how the law is written. Again and again, gay-marriage advocates have shown themselves eager to disobey any law that would prevent the spread of gay marriage from state to state. If you believe this process can be ended by anything short of a federal constitutional amendment, you are dreaming.

It took only a single day of legal gay marriage to reveal the worthlessness of assurances about this experiment's confinement to Massachusetts. Let's review the curious history of Chapter 207: Section 11, the provision of Massachusetts law that supposedly prevents the marriage of out-of-state residents whose marriages would not be legal in their home state.

When the *Goodridge* decision was handed down [in] November [2003], Justice [John M.] Greaney, who was in the majority, issued a concurring opinion containing the following claim:

> The argument, made by some in the case, that legalization of same-sex marriage in Massachusetts will be used by persons in other States as a tool to obtain recognition of a marriage in their State that is otherwise unlawful, is precluded by the provision of G.L. c. 207, 11, 12, and 13.

That law states that if your marriage would not be valid in your home state (but would be valid in Massachusetts), you can't get married in Massachusetts without actually moving to Massachusetts. Justice Greaney is clearly assuming that this law is valid, and that it should and will be enforced by state officials.

That was in November of 2003. Three months later, journalist and gay-marriage advocate Andrew Sullivan touted the same law cited by Justice Greaney as proof that "federalism works." According to Sullivan, true conservatives—those who believe in states' rights—can see that there is no need for a Federal Marriage Amendment. The residency law will prevent same-sex marriages contracted in Massachusetts from being exported to other states.

Judicial Waffling

Of course, with or without the specific approval of Justice Greaney or Andrew Sullivan, the law in question is valid in Massachusetts. So Attorney General Thomas F. Reilly announced on March 30 [2004] that the residency requirement would be enforced. At this point, however, the first bit of waffling emerged. Even though same-sex marriage is legal in no other state, Reilly would only definitively rule out marriages to same-sex couples from the 39 states with explicit laws defining marriage as the union of a man and a woman. Reilly was vague about whether marriages would be denied to residents of other states.

Governor Mitt Romney quickly filled in that gap. A spokesman for Romney explained that, since gay marriage is illegal in every other state, only Massachusetts residents would be eligible for same-sex weddings. Even so, the gray area that emerged in Reilly's statement raised the prospect that, contrary to Justice Greaney's assurances, Massachusetts marriages might indeed be "used as a tool" to obtain recognition for same-sex marriages in eleven states where such marriages were "otherwise unlawful."

Civil Disobedience

No sooner had the attorney general and the governor confirmed their intention to enforce the residency law than a torrent of criticism from gay-marriage proponents began. *Boston*

Globe columnist Derrick Jackson slammed Reilly for "buckling." The law in question had been used to prevent the export of interracial marriages to states that had once forbidden such unions. (Jackson didn't mention that the original law was also meant to cover interstate differences on things like age of minority and parental consent.) Since the residency law was a relic of the odious days of segregation, said Jackson, it was obviously discriminatory and should not be enforced.

A few weeks later, a group of Massachusetts state legislators announced an effort to repeal the residency law. That, at least, was an attempt to work through democratic and legal channels. But one of the reasons given by Representative Robert Spellane for repealing the residency requirement is telling. Spellane claimed that the law ought to go because it is discriminatory—and because it violates the *Goodridge* decision. So in just four months time, the residency requirement had morphed from something actually relied on in *Goodridge* to an outrageous piece of discrimination supposedly voided by *Goodridge*.

Next came the plans for civil disobedience. Why wait for liberal legislators to repeal the residency law when you can simply defy it? Town clerks in Provincetown, Worcester, and several other Massachusetts cities announced that they would issue marriage licenses to out-of-state couples. Then district attorneys in several localities said they would not prosecute clerks who violated the law. Norfolk County District Attorney William R. Keating said that because the original law was enacted in part to enforce prohibitions on interracial marriage, it was now effectively void. Keating made this claim, despite the fact that the original law was not about interracial marriage alone, and despite the fact that *Goodridge* itself actually relied upon the validity of the residency law.

Violating Residency Laws

And on the very first day that gay marriage was legal in Massachusetts, the residency law was in fact violated. In at least four communities, marriage licenses were issued to couples even if they said they had no intention of moving to Massachusetts. The mayor of Somerville explicitly welcomed out-of-state couples. More than a third of applications in Provincetown were from out-of-state couples. Some made it clear on their applications that they had no intention of moving to Massachusetts. Others admitted later to the *New York Times* that they'd lied about their intentions.

Bending the Law

Now let's shift from law-breaking in Massachusetts to law bending in New York. As of now, same-sex marriages cannot be legally performed in New York State. So says New York Attorney General Eliot Spitzer. Yet Spitzer has suggested to Governor Romney of Massachusetts that New York *would* recognize same-sex marriages of New York residents performed in Massachusetts. New York Governor [George] Pataki disagrees. The stage is set for conflict.

Attorney General Spitzer's position is devious and contradictory. Spitzer acknowledges that same-sex marriages cannot be legally performed in New York. So under the Massachusetts residency law, the marriage of a same-sex couple from New York must be illegal in Massachusetts as well. But Spitzer suggested that Romney should marry same-sex couples from New York in Massachusetts (so that Spitzer can then recognize their marriages in New York). In effect, Spitzer is using Massachusetts marriages to make an end-run around his own state's laws. So with the connivance of New York State's own attorney general, same-sex marriage is in fact being "used as a tool" to obtain recognition of a marriage that would "otherwise be unlawful."

In other words, the very thing that Justice Greaney assured us would not happen is in fact happening. Civil disobedience by public officials in Massachusetts is opening up marriage to out-of-state couples. And legal manipulation by officials in

New York is being used to obtain recognition for same-sex marriages when no legislative or even judicial action legalizing such unions has been taken in New York. . . .

Again and again, however, the law is being violated. In San Francisco, in Sandoval County (New Mexico), in New Paltz (New York), and in Asbury Park (New Jersey), local officials have systematically defied the law. The mayor of New Paltz has lately been in court facing criminal charges for solemnizing marriages without licenses. And even as he called on conservatives to uphold federalism, Andrew Sullivan touted San Francisco's flagrant defiance of California law.

When it comes to same-sex marriage, federalism can't work—because the advocates of same-sex marriage won't let it work. Andrew Sullivan can't credibly ask conservatives not to worry about the export of Massachusetts marriages when he himself supported open defiance of California law by the mayor of San Francisco. Massachusetts's Justice Greaney cannot credibly ask opponents of same-sex marriage not to worry about the export of Massachusetts marriages when officials of his own state systematically violate the very law that he points to.

Need for a Federal Marriage Amendment

We're told the law doesn't matter here, because it's a question of fundamental civil rights. But that's the problem. The reason activist judges have usurped the legislative role on this issue is that they, too, see the question as one of fundamental civil rights. Any judge can void any state marriage law on grounds of equal protection or due process. Equal-protection and due-process claims have the potential to void Defense of Marriage Act statutes, and an equal-protection or due-process finding by the United States Supreme Court could overturn even marriage amendments to all 50 state constitutions.

So the civil-rights analogy makes the issue of same-sex marriage impossible to resolve by federalist principles. If gay marriage is really an issue of fundamental civil rights, you can't let some states prohibit it while others allow it. And gay-marriage advocates—be they private individuals, municipal officials, or judges—do see the issue as a question of fundamental civil rights. For that reason, they will defy or overturn any law that gets in their way.

Events have already made it clear that on the question of same-sex marriage, it's going to be all or nothing. Either we are going to have same-sex marriage everywhere, or we are going to have a Federal Marriage Amendment. After only a single day, assurances that federalism can work on this issue have proved hollow.

Organizations to Contact

The editors have compiled the following list of organizations concerned with the issues debated in this book. The descriptions are derived from materials provided by the organizations. All have publications or information available for interested readers. The list was compiled on the date of publication of the present volume; the information provided here may change. Be aware that many organizations take several weeks or longer to respond to inquiries, so allow as much time as possible.

American Civil Liberties Union (ACLU) Lesbian Gay Bisexual Transgender and AIDS Project
125 Broad St., New York, NY   10004
(212) 549-2627
Web site: www.aclu.org/getequal

Founded in 1920, the ACLU is dedicated to defending the constitutional rights of all Americans, in court and in legislatures, and is one of the nation's best-known civil rights organizations. In 1986, it launched the Lesbian Gay Bisexual Transgender and AIDS Project, which undertakes cases specifically focused on gay rights issues. In addition to its legal work, the project provides materials and assistance to gay parents, gay youth, and those struggling with gender identity, as well as to people facing discrimination because of their HIV status.

Concerned Women for America (CWA)
1015 Fifteenth St. NW, Suite 1100, Washington, DC   20005
(202) 488-7000 • fax: (202) 488-0806
Web site: www.cwfa.org

The nation's largest public policy women's organization, the CWA is devoted to promoting biblical values throughout society, through prayer, education, and political activism. Its Culture and Family Institute is particularly focused on protecting traditional ideas of the family from perceived threats, including the gay rights movement. It does this through lobbying, working with media outlets, and providing educational materials to schools and individuals.

Focus on the Family
Colorado Springs, CO   80995
(800) 232-6459
Web site: www.family.org

Focus on the Family was founded in 1977 by James Dobson as a Christian nonprofit organization. Its mission is to defend the traditional family against perceived threats from political activists and social progressives, including gay rights organizations. It works with churches across denominational lines to provide a united voice against abortion, homosexuality, the teaching of evolution, and premarital sex, and in favor of school prayer and corporal punishment. It also broadcasts a national talk radio show, hosted by Dobson, and publishes numerous books and magazines.

Human Rights Campaign (HRC)
1640 Rhode Island Ave. NW, Washington, DC   20036-3278
(800) 777-4723 • fax: (202) 347-5323
Web site: www.hrc.org

Founded in 1980 and now America's largest gay rights organization, the HRC lobbies legislators, advocates in the media, and provides educational materials designed to further the struggle for gay rights. Information on same-sex marriage, gays in the military, workplace issues, and numerous other causes of interest to gay, lesbian, bisexual, and transgendered people can all be found on the HRC Web site.

Lambda Legal Defense and Education Fund
120 Wall St., Suite 1500, New York, NY   10005-3904
(212) 809-8585 • fax (212) 809-0055
Web site: www.lambdalegal.com

Working primarily through litigation, Lambda Legal has the goal of achieving full civil rights for gay, lesbian, bisexual, and transgendered people, and for people who are HIV positive. It also maintains a roster of volunteer attorneys and legal practitioners willing to help pursue test cases in every region of the country. It publishes numerous educational materials, including booklets, fact sheets, and *Lambda Legal Update*. Lambda Legal maintains offices in New York, Los Angeles, Chicago, Atlanta, and Dallas.

Marriage Equality USA
4096 Piedmont Ave. Suite 257, Oakland, CA   94611
(510) 496-2700 • fax: (510) 380-5200
Web site: www.marriageequality.org

Founded in 1998, Marriage Equality is dedicated to establishing marriage rights for gay couples and families. It organizes demonstrations, helps build grassroots local organizations, and provides speakers and materials. It also launches letter-writing campaigns, speak-outs, and other media campaigns to familiarize the public with the issue and the difficulties faced by gay couples seeking the same legal status as straight couples.

National Gay and Lesbian Task Force (NGLTF)
1325 Massachusetts Ave. NW, Suite 600
Washington, DC   20005
(202) 393-5177 • fax: (202) 393-2241
Web site: www.thetaskforce.org

America's oldest gay rights organization, the NGLTF was founded in 1973. It continues to serve as a leader in grassroots organizing, lobbying federal and state legislatures and agencies, and training activists. It seeks full equality for gay people in the military, the workplace, schools, and communities. It also organizes the annual Creating Change Conference, which attracts upwards of two thousand activists and members of the media interested in gay rights issues. In addition to its Washington headquarters, NGLTF has regional offices throughout the country.

Traditional Values Coalition (TVC)
139 C St. SE, Washington, DC   20003
(202) 547-8570 • fax: (202) 546-6403
Web site: www.traditionalvalues.org

TVC was founded in 1980 by Rev. Lou Sheldon, the author of *The Agenda: The Homosexual Plan to Change America*. It has become one of the largest and most influential organizations opposing the acceptance of homosexuality and defending traditional family values. It also encourages political participation by conservative churches and pastors, especially through its Traditional Values Coalition Education and Legal Institute. Its Web site provides numerous materials for those seeking to oppose homosexuality or their own same-sex attractions.

For Further Research

Books

Robert M. Baird and M. Katherine Baird, *Homosexuality: Debating the Issues*. Amherst, NY: Prometheus Books, 1995.

Patricia M. Cain, *Rainbow Rights: The Role of Lawyers and Courts in the Lesbian and Gay Civil Rights Movement*. Boulder, CO: Westview Press, 2001.

Donald J. Cantor et al., *Same-Sex Marriage: The Legal and Psychological Evolution in America*. Middleton, CT: Wesleyan University Press, 2006.

George Chauncey, *Why Marriage? The History Shaping Today's Debate over Gay Equality*. New York: Basic Books, 2004.

Stephen Michael Cretney, *Same-Sex Relationships: From "Odious Crime" to "Gay Marriage."* New York: Oxford University Press, 2006.

William N. Eskridge, *Gay Marriage: For Better or for Worse? What We've Learned from the Evidence*. New York: Oxford University Press, 2006.

Evan Gerstmann, *Same-Sex Marriage and the Constitution*. New York: Cambridge University Press, 2004.

D. James Kennedy and Jerry Newcombe, *What's Wrong with Same-Sex Marriage?* Wheaton, IL: Crossway Books, 2004.

Andrew Koppelman, *The Gay Rights Question in Contemporary American Law*. Chicago: University of Chicago Press, 2002.

Eric Marcus, *Making History: The Struggle for Gay and Lesbian Equal Rights, 1945–1990*. New York: HarperCollins, 1992.

Joyce Murdoch and Deb Price, *Courting Justice: Gay Men and Lesbians v. the Supreme Court*. New York: Basic Books, 2001.

Saul M. Olyan and Martha Nussbaum, *Sexual Orientation and Human Rights in American Religious Discourse*. New York: Oxford University Press, 1988.

Jason Pierceson, *Courts, Liberalism and Rights: Gay Law and Politics in the United States and Canada*. Philadelphia: Temple University Press, 2005.

Jonathan Rauch, *Gay Marriage: Why It Is Good for Gays, Good for Straights, and Good for America*. New York: Henry Holt, 2004.

David A. J. Richards, *The Case for Gay Rights: From Bowers to Lawrence and Beyond*. Lawrence: University Press of Kansas, 2005.

Andrew Sullivan, ed., *Same-Sex Marriage: Pro and Con*. New York: Vintage Books, 1997.

Stephanie L. Witt and Suzanne McCorkle, eds., *Anti-Gay Rights: Assessing Voter Initiatives*. Westport, CT: Praeger, 1997.

Periodicals

Carlos A. Ball, "The Positive in the Fundamental Right to Marry: Same-Sex Marriage in the Aftermath of *Lawrence v. Texas*," *Minnesota Law Review*, 2004.

Robert H. Bork, "The Necessary Amendment," *First Things*, August/September 2004.

William F. Buckley, "Gay Impasse," *National Review*, October 27, 2006.

Chris Bull, "Continuing Milk's Legacy," *Advocate*, November 11, 2003.

Susan Burgess, "Queer (Theory) Eye for the Straight (Legal) Guy: *Lawrence v. Texas*' Makeover of *Bowers v. Hardwick*," *Political Research Quarterly*, vol. 59, no. 3, 2006.

Dale Carpenter, "The Unknown Past of *Lawrence v. Texas*," *Michigan Law Review*, June 1, 2004.

David Orgon Coolidge and William C. Duncan, "Reaffirming Marriage: A Presidential Priority," *Harvard Journal of Law & Public Policy*, Spring 2001.

Elizabeth B. Cooper, "Who Needs Marriage? Equality and the Role of the State," *Journal of Law & Family Studies*, November 16, 2006.

Barney Frank, "Civil Rights, Legislative Wrongs," *Advocate*, February 15, 2000.

Katherine M. Franke, "The Politics of Same-Sex Marriage Politics," *Columbia Journal of Gender and Law*, vol. 15, 2006.

Jamal Greene, "Beyond *Lawrence*: Metaprivacy and Punishment," *Yale Law Journal*, vol. 115, 2006.

Peter Heinegg, "Gay Rights for Christians?" *Cross Currents*, Winter 2005.

Kay S. Hymowitz, "I Do?" *Commentary*, June 2004.

Ebony "Is Gay Rights a Civil Rights Issue?" July 2004.

Thomas M. Keck, "Queering the Rehnquist Court," *Political Research Quarterly*, September 1, 2006.

Richard Kim, "Queer Cheer," *Nation*, July 21, 2003.

Michael Klarman, "*Brown* and *Lawrence* (and *Goodridge*)," *Michigan Law Review*, December 1, 2005.

Judith E. Koons, "'Just' Married? Same-Sex Marriage and a History of Family Plurality," *Michigan Journal of Gender & Law*, vol. 12, no. 1, 2005.

Robert Justin Lipkin, "The Harm of Same-Sex Marriage: Real or Imagined?" *Widener Law Review*, vol. 11, no. 2, 2005.

Christopher Lisotta, "Courting Discrimination," *Advocate*, April 13, 2004.

Jay Michaelson, "On Listening to the Kulturkampf, or How America Overruled *Bowers v. Hardwick*, Even Though *Romer v. Evans* Didn't," *Duke Law Journal*, April 1, 2000.

Norman Podhoretz, "How the Gay-Rights Movement Won," *Commentary*, November 1996.

Justin Raimondo, "A Gay Man Decries 'Gay Rights,'" *American Enterprise*, March 1, 2000.

Regent University Law Review "Symposium: Moral Realism and the Renaissance of Traditional Marriage," vol. 17, 2004/2005.

Eric Reid, "Assessing and Responding to Same-Sex 'Marriage' in Light of Natural Law," *Georgetown Journal of Law & Public Policy*, Summer 2005.

Vincent J. Samar, "Privacy and the Debate over Same-Sex Marriage Versus Unions," *DePaul Law Review*, June 2005.

Alicia Shepard, "Did the Networks Sanitize the Gay Rights March?" *American Journalism Review*, July 1993.

Thomas Short, "Gay Rights or Closet Virtues?" *National Review*, September 17, 1990.

Fred Smith, "Gendered Justice: Do Male and Female Judges Rule Differently on Questions of Gay Rights?" *Stanford Law Review*, vol. 57, 2005.

Bonnie Spanier, "Biological Determinism and Homosexuality," *NWSA Journal*, vol. 7, 1995.

J. Stoutenborough, D. Haider-Markel and M. Allen, "Reassessing the Impact of Supreme Court Decisions on Public Opinion: Gay Civil Rights Cases," *Political Research Quarterly*, vol. 59, no. 3, 2006.

Andrew Sullivan, "Quite Contrary," *New Republic*, December 25, 2006.

Eugene Volokh, "Same-Sex Marriage and Slippery Slopes," *Hofstra Law Review*, October 5, 2005.

David M. Wagner, "Gay Marriage Lite," *Weekly Standard*, November 6, 2006.

John Woolman, "Letter from a Friend: A Conservative Speaks Out for Gay Rights," *National Review*, September 12, 1986.

Index